July 203

Dear Terri and Butch

A little bit of ~~~~ with

you on your ~~~~

All the best -
with love -
Susan

A London Cabbie...

I would like to thank and acknowledge:

All the cabbies who helped and encouraged me
to write this book. I hope that it will be a testimony
to my dear friend Ralph who sadly passed away before
it went to print.

To my grandfather, Joseph, who on my seventh
birthday gave me my first camera, taught me the
secrets of the 'photographic eye'.

To my two boys, Ibby and Kem,
who kept my computer running.

To Caroline Walsh, the passenger I met as if by kismet,
who took up my work, became my agent
and made it possible to get this book published.

To the people I have met in my cab as they
'journey through life', even only for a few moments
sharing part of it with me.

And lastly to the city that I love, the place where
I was born, that is life itself, has made me what I am,
a London cabbie, 'I will leave my light on for you'…

A London Cabbie...

In a Year

of a London Cabbie

Everyone has a Story

ORION

I dedicate this book

To my parents who gave me life

And

To the teacher who did not

Believe in me ...

Who I am,
What I look like,
Isn't important.
But for my badge number, 42629,
Could be one
Of any 23,000 London cabbies
With a story to tell.
This is my story.
Took nine months to write.
No other cabbie has attempted it before,
Pictures and stories
Mostly taken
From the seat of my cab.
You will see
What I see through my eyes,
Passing shadows in the street,
The passengers,
And the cabbies too,
The feelings,
The buzz
That makes London what it is,
That makes me what I am.

I was raised
By my parents
Who owned a fruit and vegetable shop
Near Highgate.
Went to a local school.
My teacher would tell me
My English was 'pathetic'.
This scarred me for life,
Never passed an English exam.
Then by the age of nineteen
I gave up my dream
Of going to university.

Got a job as a bank clerk,
Worked several years
As a computer operator,
Ended up pressing ladies'
garments
In a factory in the East End.

Then, got on a moped,
Rode 9,000 miles
In fifteen months
Completed the knowledge.
I got my badge
Became a London cabbie.

One day, unexpectedly,
Met an old couple
From Euston station,
Told me a lovely story.
Didn't want to lose it,
Had to write it down,
And with a photo
Froze that moment in time
For ever.

Let's begin,
Let's enjoy the journey…

It's spring

Here in London.

Tavistock Square is in blossom.

A woman

With a young child

Passes beneath the Tree of Peace.

I look at my watch

Time to start my day.

I finish my coffee,

Switch on my yellow hire light,

Head to Euston station,

Find the 9.40 train hasn't arrived.

A long queue of cabbies are waiting

For passengers.

Some are reading papers,

Others get out

To stretch their legs,

An excuse to have a morning chat.

This is all a bit early for me.

I relax for a moment,

Roll back into my seat,

Think of a night

Several years ago,

It was a pleasant trip.

A pleasant trip

I was driving down Camden High Street on a Saturday night. It was about 12.30 a.m., I felt tired, decided to go home. I switched off my hire light, when I noticed a middle-aged city gent, smartly dressed, must have had a few drinks. He came staggering out of Camden Palace into the road and forced me to brake hard. Before I could give him a piece of my mind, he jumped in.

'Palmers Green,' he said. Now I could have refused him, but he looked desperate – anyway it was near where I lived.

'I'll take you,' I said. Switched on my meter, not another word was said. Eventually I got home at 1.15 a.m., locked the cab in the garage and went straight to bed. I dozed off when suddenly thoughts passed by me. 'What happened to the man in my cab?'

I opened my eyes, jumped out of bed, slipped on my slippers and dressing gown, and ran down the stairs to the garage. I unlocked the doors, found the meter running and this man sleeping in the back of the cab. What have I done? I reversed the cab, out of the driveway, on to the road, got him quickly home and woke him up.

He got out, paid me with a tip: 'Pleasant trip.'

Not another word was said.

CAMDEN HIGH STREET TO PALMERS GREEN

At our age you don't rush any more

A cab blasts his horn, almost jolts me from my seat.
The train has arrived. Passengers are rushing down the steps.
The cabs are on the move. I pick up an elderly couple.
Their destination is Paddington. I know the journey is going
to be slow, as the Marylebone Road is congested with traffic,
and I apologise in advance for the delay.

'No problem, we have plenty of time. At our age you don't
rush any more,' the old man said.

I then took the opportunity to ask how they had met and,
as I expected, he gave me a smile and told me a tale.

'I am eighty-four years old this year, met my wife during the
Second World War. She was a hairdresser then, giving us lads
a short back and sides. The first time I met her, I knew she
was the lady for me. When she gave me another haircut,
several weeks later, I asked her out and she accepted. But it
was hard in those days, the war, the Blitz, she kept me going
when I thought it was the end.' He explained, 'You see, I was
an officer in the 60th Airborne Division, there were three
squadrons of forty men. That day, 6 June 1944, D-Day, when
we were amongst the first to be dropped in Normandy, was a
day when I was scared, yet excited to do a job we were sent to
do. Within the first hour twenty paras were captured, many
were killed, and I am lucky to be here to tell the tale.'

He told me that each year on 9 September he meets the
survivors at the Victory Club, Seymour Street. He took out
his wallet, took out a little sticker with their name and
address and passed it to me through the window. I put it
immediately into my folder so I wouldn't lose it.

I arrived at Paddington more quickly than I had expected
that day, and that was unusual. What was more, they agreed
to some photos, something I had never asked anyone to do
before. They agreed happily. I thanked them and we parted.

EUSTON STATION TO PADDINGTON STATION

At our age
you don't rush
any more

We have an insight

Into people's lives

Because we pick them up,

Listen to them

Without prejudice,

Like a padre at confession,

Knowing when they leave

We won't see them again.

A day in spring

She told me she was in love.
'That's special,' I said.
'But it's hard to describe those feelings,' she replied.

I know exactly what she meant. I too tried once to put
those feelings into words. I recited them to her:

I am the paint,
You are the painting,
I am the ink,
You are the words,
I am a star,
You are the universe.
When I look at you
I see a painting,
With pretty colours
Of a rainbow,
See an angel,
See a woman,
See a mother
With a newborn child,
How beautiful it is!

Then
When I look into your eyes
Words flow through my mind,
Like sweet waters of a stream,
Is this magic?
This is poetry –
What is happening to me?

And then,
When I look into your heart,
See the universe,
See the stars,
See a soul
That's burning with passion
As it fades towards
The sun,
What are these feelings
That I see?

Is it because?
I am the paint,
You are the painting,
I am the ink,
You are the words,
I am a star
And you my love,
You are the universe …

PADDINGTON STATION TO ISLINGTON

12

My head is like a magnet

'Whenever I'm tired I always hit my head on the cab door, it's like a magnet. It's not that it's painful, it's just embarrassing. People must look at me and think what a prat I am.'

'Sir, it happens all the time, that's why I always carry some spare aspirins.'

CHARING CROSS STATION TO GRAY'S INN ROAD

An Irish joke

'I am from Dublin, I will tell you an Irish joke. There is this man called Paddy, he is stopped by a Garda patrol car. He gets out of his car wondering what's wrong. The Garda notices a glazed look, a smell of alcohol upon Paddy's breath, he questions him.

"Have you been drinking?"

"Doing nothing else all day," Paddy says. "Started at 11 a.m. at O'Neill's in Suffolk Street, had four pints there. Then met up with couple of mates at Johnny Fox's, shared a bottle of whiskey, had a great lunch there. Then at 5 p.m. we all went to O'Donoghue's to watch a match on the big satellite screen, had fifteen pints of Guinness …"

'The Garda interrupts, "In that case you better blow into this bag."

'"What's the problem, you don't believe me?"'

I won her with a five-shilling bet

'The Sixties were great days in Liverpool – the music, the Beatles and other stars who became famous were just names then.

'I was a Teddy boy then and when I went to a disco at the Mersey View Bar with a mate to hear this music I saw this girl standing with her mates at the bar. Now she was nice, and I wanted to dance with her. My mate dared me with a five-shilling bet to go over and ask her for a dance, but I couldn't. The night dragged on and then the DJ put on a slow record called 'Save the last dance for me'. I put my fears behind me, went over, and asked her for that dance, and she accepted.

'I won her with a five-shilling bet that night, got off with her but nothing happened – we were only kids, she fifteen and I seventeen. That was thirty-nine years ago and we have been together ever since.'

George and Pam been married now for thirty-five years, have five children and eight grandchildren, and live happily together in Cheshire.

EUSTON STATION TO WEMBLEY

The Norwegian way

'We are from Bergen, Norway, the land
of fjords and beautiful mountains.
We have come to London, we're having
a great holiday and find the people friendly.

'We met "the Norwegian way", on a ski
slope. I noticed her in front of me and told
her, "Hurry up, you're too slow."

'So she did. We have been together
for sixteen years.'

SLOANE STREET TO BUTLER'S WHARF

The best girl I've ever met

'I am a student from Lucerne, Switzerland. This is a portrait of a girl
who was in the same musical cast as I was. She was in love with me, I was
in love with her. But neither of us dared to get in touch with each other.

'But then we had to play a love scene and both of us suddenly realised
that we were more than just "playing" a love scene. The scene was
'The Sun' in the show *Metropolis*. She was the soprano (Maria)
and I was the tenor (Steven).

'We are now together and she is the best girl I've ever met in my life.'

UXBRIDGE ROAD TO SUTTON COURT ROAD

Very much in love

'One Friday night I was going to meet some mates for a drink, but I couldn't contact them by telephone. I almost went home but decided to make something of a bad situation and go to my old bar, the Metro in Oxford Street.

'When I used to go there six months earlier, I saw this girl. I always tried to date her, but each time she turned me down, making a fool of me in front of my mates. On this night when I was there by chance, without my mates, I wanted to enjoy the night. Then I saw that girl sitting alone on a table, and I thought I'd try my luck.

'This time she accepted my invitation, but I didn't have a pen to write her telephone number down. So I rushed to the bar, interrupted this woman talking to her friend, got a pen and wrote her number down on my hand. Later I realised, after I returned the pen, that I had only six digits of her number. So I went back to the woman at the bar for the pen, but this time noticed how attractive she was. We hit off with a conversation straight away. She told me how she had accompanied her friend there by chance to interview three bands.

'Yes, it was by chance we both were there, and we've been dating since. We are now both very much in love.'

OXFORD STREET TO KING'S CROSS STATION

She sorted it out

'I am a Scot, married to a Bulgarian, living in India – how about that!

'We've just spent a few days' holiday in Barcelona, and decided we must come to London before returning back home to India.

'I used to work in Bulgaria – lived in this luxurious rented villa in Sofia. I employed a gardener but then the landlord decided to replace him with a relative, which caused a disagreement, Since we had a language problem an interpreter was brought in to help mediate. Now she was an attractive woman, she sorted it out and I felt I needed to know her better. Funny as it may sound, she later became my wife.

'We moved to Moscow, but at −25°C it was a bit too cold, so when asked if we wanted somewhere warmer we said yes and landed up in Bombay.'

Nice story, I thought, before we parted at the Sloane Club. I recommended them not to miss the spectacular views of London 450 feet up from the London Eye, but told them to be sure to go to a lavatory first because it's a forty-minute ride.

EUSTON STATION TO THE SLOANE CLUB

A morning in Tottenham Court Road

Playing footsie under the table

'When I was a student, I went to a friend's party. There, as we sat having dinner I started playing footsie under the table.

'I didn't know whose feet they were, so I looked under the table and so did she. When we saw each other we both crawled under the table, kissed and that was the beginning of a romance.

'The next day I called her father, told him, "I would like to know your daughter" and that was it. We have now been married for thirty-five years. We have come to London from the USA and are having a great time.'

OXFORD STREET TO THE STRAND

From Russia with love

21

'We are from Moscow, Russia. We are businessmen come here to buy some Skoda parts. This is our first visit to England. We like your country. The people here are very friendly and you must visit us some day.

'Let's write our names down for you.'

EUSTON STATION TO KING'S CROSS ROAD

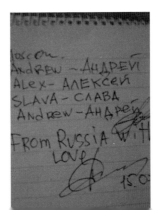

April showers

I was driving along Camberwell New Road when I saw two people running across, waving to me to stop, so I did. They got in, soaked.

'We've been walking in the pouring rain from a friend's house to our house, only to find we have left our keys behind. We are wet, tired and annoyed. We had a long walk back to our friend's house to get our keys. Then we saw your hire light. Cabbie, you're a godsend.'

CAMBERWELL NEW ROAD TO CLAPHAM ROAD

I like London
even when it rains.

A £1.00 bet

'My friend and I have come down to London for our friend's father's memorial service at St Clement's church (the RAF church). He was a pilot taken prisoner during the Second World War and detained in one of the notorious Stalag prison camps. He is the only one of fourteen ever to have escaped. Now what are the chances of that?

'I will tell you another story. I work in an office that had a seven-man lottery syndicate, each one giving £1.00 per week. One Friday one of them decides to pull out and I am accepted as a replacement. On Saturday next day in the evening I get an unexpected phone call. We have just won £3,500,000 (£500,000 each) on the Lottery. I am a very happy man, having won £500,000 with a £1.00 bet. Now what are the chances of that?

'On Monday I go back to work. The other winners have taken a day off work and the only other person there is the one who pulled out from the syndicate a few days earlier. He asks me, "Where is everyone?"

'"Didn't you know?" I say. "We won £3,500,000 from the Lottery on Saturday."'

EUSTON STATION TO ST CLEMENT'S CHURCH

Meet Molly Malone

'My dog is my best friend. She is six years old and is called Molly Malone because she lives near Portobello market. She is on her way back from the office. She loves typing and bargain hunting on Fridays in the market.'

When we got to our destination there was a friend waiting for her.

WESTBOURNE GROVE TO LADBROKE GROVE

Ralph

'Good morning, my name is Ralph. I can forget about the traffic and the rain now and have my breakfast here at the Granby Gril in NW1. Inside it's bustling with life. My cabbie friends congregate here, chat noisily about their experiences and stories they've heard in the streets of this city. Let's go in and taste the experience.

'Take a seat, make yourself comfortable. While waiting for my breakfast I will tell you something about us cabbies.

'To be accepted as a London cabbie you have to do the "Knowledge". You must be of good character without any criminal convictions, have a clean licence and have a medical to prove that you are physically fit for the job. Only if you meet these criteria will you be considered as an applicant. The Knowledge is a blue book, with over 400 runs (routes), which the candidate, often on a moped, will go out, learn and memorise if he or she is to have any chance of qualifying. The area comprises 25,000 streets within a six-mile radius of Charing Cross station. Having learnt these streets you are also required to know the hospitals, clubs, government buildings, railway stations, courts and about every other building or institution you can imagine. Once you have passed this, done a further sixty runs in the suburbs, hopefully all within three years, you are then given a difficult driving test. Only then do you qualify and get given your badge.

Taste the experience at the Granby Grill

'But some applicants never make it. Some have nervous breakdowns, like an applicant I remember who could not take the pressure during an oral examination, grabbed the examiner by the throat and tried to strangle him. He was dismissed on the spot – not surprising, I thought.

'London cabs are purpose-built vehicles to carry the public. They are distinctive in design, can turn on a sixpence and can take the punishment that is demanded of them.

'London cabs have been in this city since the seventeenth century and it was not until 1654 that Oliver Cromwell passed an Act of Parliament that made driving a London cab a recognised profession.

'The London licensed taxis trade is unique. There is no other city where you can get into a cab and feel confident that the driver knows exactly where he's going.

'Over the years I've got to know a lot of cabbies. To hear them talk, especially when they are sitting together over a mug of tea in a café, is an experience you won't forget.

Their charisma, the way they express themselves – they're like actors in front of a large audience. They'll keep you in suspense all night with their stories.

'Cabbies have good "communication skills", can make conversation quickly with passengers. They are good listeners, they express themselves well and they make natural counsellors. Also, because they are streetwise, they have insight, often sensing trouble before it happens. They can tell a lot about a person before they get in their cab. In short, they have a sixth sense.

Many cabbies are creative, and having done the Knowledge they have good memories. They can remember faces of passengers, their conversations, where they dropped them off even if it was several years ago. They would make wonderful detectives.

'A cabbie has unlimited knowledge at his fingertips. If he wants free medical advice he needs only to go down

Harley Street after 5 p.m., where there's a good chance of picking up a consultant, for legal advice Middle Lane or any court like the Royal Courts of Justice in the Strand, for financial advice the City – the list goes on. Speaking to passengers broadens a cabbie's knowledge of life. None of this costs him a penny – in fact they pay him.

'Anyone who underestimates a cabbie is making a mistake. There's cabbies like Fred Housego who won *Mastermind*, Peter Shreeves who became manager of Sheffield Wednesday, Brian Hall who became an actor in the television series *Fawlty Towers* and I know many who have taken degrees and written novels. Cabbies are unique and I am proud to be one of them.

'Then there's the gridlock in traffic. I often watch motorists and cyclists getting stressed, probably getting ulcers, passengers looking at their watches telling me they are late for an appointment, a train, etc. Why get excited, nothing you can do about it, so why get worked up? For them, stuck in traffic, they're losing time, money. But for a cabbie, he's not losing anything because he is already there. He is on time the moment he gets into his cab.

'Then, when I want to, I just switch off my light, go to the Granby Grill for a tea or take a stroll in Regent's Park. In how many professions can you do that?'

Cabology

The Knowledge is the course you are required to do to become a London licensed black cab driver.

A Knowledge boy or girl is someone doing the Knowledge.

To be on the foul is to exceed the number of cabs allowed on any one rank.

To broom off someone is to refuse to take a passenger.

A butter boy is a new cab driver.

To bilk someone is to defraud a cab driver of his or her fare.

A musher is an owner-driver.

A legal is a customer who pays only the fare displayed on the meter, without giving a tip.

A face is a cabbie who specialises in airport and hotel runs.

A taxi is a vehicle fitted with a meter.

The Yard is the Carriage Office in Penton Street.

The kipper season is the time of year when trade is quiet (usually January, February and March).

The Wedding Cake is the Queen Victoria Memorial at the bottom of the Mall, next to Buckingham Palace.

The Magic Roundabout is Shepherd's Bush.

The Wall of Death is the Rotunda at the junction of London Wall, St Martin's le Grand and Aldersgate Street.

The Gasworks is the Houses of Parliament.

The Glasshouse is the reception at the Barbican Centre.

The Horse's Tail is the statue of General Napier on his horse at the junction of Queen's Gate and Kensington Gore.

Little Ben is the clock tower on the island in Victoria Street opposite Victoria bus station.

The Hole in the Wall is the entrance to Victoria Station from Wilton Road.

The Shakespeare or Shakes is a pub in Buckingham Palace Road where passengers ask to be dropped off for Victoria Station.

A journeyman is a cabbie who works for someone else, i.e. hires a cab.

A leatherarse is a cabbie who works long hours.

A stalker is a cabbie who doesn't put the meter on.

'Be lucky' are the traditional words said when cabbies part.

It is customary for a cabbie on his very first job to give a passenger a free ride.

Lady Godiva	£5
Big Ben	£10
Cock and Hen	£25
Nifty	£50
Ton	£100
Monkey	£500

Meet some cab

Bernie

'My name is Bernie. In 1968, one Saturday morning at about 8 a.m., I got an urgent radio job to take a man with his wife, who was in labour, to St George's Hospital at Hyde Park Corner.

'By the time we had reached Belgrave Square, her contractions were every minute. Her water broke, she started screaming and he panicked. With the baby's head appearing, I knew I had to act quickly, so I stopped the cab, got into the back, pulled my sleeves up and slowly helped ease the baby out.

'She gave birth to a baby boy in my cab and what a moment it was! She asked me my name, then shortly afterwards a doctor arrived in an ambulance, congratulated me, told me I did a good job.

'The boy will be thirty-two years old now. I sometimes wonder what his name is. Where he is in life? Maybe I have had him in my cab – God knows ...'

Bernie is from Essex. He is married with two children and four grandchildren. He has been a cabbie now for forty-two years.

Edward

'I was driving in the pouring rain and had stopped at the red lights at South Kensington, when I heard my back doors slam shut and then a ferocious argument. I turned around to find a man and woman in the back of my cab, both soaking wet, arguing. What was going on, I thought? I tried to remain patient.

'"I got in the cab first…" the man said.

'The woman interrupted, "No you didn't, you liar, I did."

'Then they started arguing again, as if I wasn't there. I didn't believe what was happening. Then I lost my cool. "Stop it," I yelled.

'Then they stopped, and since they were both going to Regent Street they reluctantly agreed to share the cab, for they knew cabs were hard to find on a wet day. When we got to Hyde Park I noticed in my mirror that they were talking to each other and making jokes. Amazing, I thought. The lady got out first, at Regent Street, followed by the gentleman at Oxford Circus.

'"I got her telephone number,' he said to me with a smile.

'Unbelievable, I thought. Then he gave me a £50 note for a £12.60 fare. "Keep the change cabbie, you deserve it."'

A sketch I drew of Edward reading his newspaper at the Granby.

Polish Michael

This is 'Polish Michael', one of the nicest cabbies you will ever meet and probably the oldest. He was born in Poland, taken prisoner in the Second World War by the Russians. He was later released and with the Polish army he joined up with the British 8th Army in the Middle East. He fought in north Africa under Montgomery and in May 1944 fought at Cassino, Italy, for which he was awarded the Bronze Medal of Merit. He is now seventy-six years old, has been driving a cab for forty-one years and loves going twice a week to a gym for an hour's workout.

Michael is happily married with two sons and four grandchildren.

In 1999 after sixty years Michael returned to Silesia, Poland, the place where he was born.

Jackie

'I have been a cabbie for thirty-seven years. Never forget a job I did nine years ago. I was just finishing a night shift when I thought I would do one more job. Picked up this young man from Holland Road. As he got into my cab something fell out of his pocket.

'He quizzed me, "Did you see what that was?"

'"Yes, a heavy lighter," I said, but I was sure it was a handgun of some sort.

'Nothing more was said about it. I took him to the bureau de change at the junction of Bayswater and Queensway, then en route to Islington he produced a radio scanner and started listening for police messages. I thought this a bit suspicious. He began talking about his girlfriend. "I am going to kill her when I find her." I began to feel nervous, but I've been a cabbie for a long time and experience has taught me to remain cool. I took him to Islington, where he started looking for a mini, but he couldn't find it. I gave a sigh of relief. Then he asked me to take him to St James's, Piccadilly, where I dropped him off.

'After that I went home, having finished a long shift, and told my wife what had happened. I thought nothing more about it, and went to bed. After several hours my wife woke me and told me that a cabbie had been shot dead in his cab. I immediately thought that there might be a connection, so I rang the police and gave them an account of my story with a description of this man. Within three days he was arrested. He was tried at the Old Bailey and consequently sentenced to sixteen years in prison for murder. The CID came back to me and told me I was very lucky to be alive.'

Jackie lives in north London. He is happily married with two daughters.

A joke heard at the Granby Grill
(told by a Jewish cabbie)

This cabbie picks up two passengers
from Russell Square. One is a rabbi,
the other a Roman Catholic
archbishop. They are on their way
to an ecumenism council. The cabbie
eavesdrops their conversation.
The archbishop asks, 'Tell me, Rabbi,
have you ever had a bacon sandwich?'

'As it happens, I have when I was
young,' the rabbi replies. 'And you,
Archbishop, have you ever had sex?'

'As it happens, I have.'

'Is it as good as a bacon sandwich?'

Meet some

Malcolm

'Once I picked up this young
woman from the City, got
into a conversation and
turned my head while
speaking.

'"Sorry," she said, "but could
you please repeat what you
just said? I can read your lips
in the mirror."

'Read my lips, I thought?
Then it dawned on me that
she must be deaf, that
throughout the whole trip
she had been reading my lips
in the driving mirror.

'She confirmed my guess.
"Funny as it may sound, I
enjoy going to see live bands
on stage, although I cannot
hear them I can feel the
thumps and vibrations."'

Malcolm has been cabbing
for thirty-three years.
He lives in Edgware,
and is happily married
with three children.

Stanley

'Thirty-five years ago, at 2 a.m. one Sunday morning after I had dropped off this man in Chiswick High Road I found this small bag in the back of my cab. I examined the contents to find:

- four French letters (two used)
- a pair of tights
- a pair of silk knickers
- a negligee
- half a bottle of perfume.

'As a good cabbie I took the lost property to Hammersmith police station. The sergeant on duty told me not to waste his time, so I left. After removing the used items, I took the rest to a market and sold them to this lady for 40 shillings, which was good money in those days.'

Stanley, who likes to tell his stories over a cup of tea, has been driving a cab for forty years. He lives in Ruislip, and is married with four children and eight grandchildren.

'Now listen to this story …'

'Would you believe that?'

Meet some **cabbies**

'Heard this joke the other day …'

Blimey, George, they are digging up the Strand again.'

'Yes, didn't you know, Bob, it's because
they've forgot where they left their shovels.'

'Here we go again ...'

'Sorry, can't repeat this one.'

'I'm Johnny,
what are you
laughing at?'

cabbies

B&Q

'I was driving over Waterloo Bridge when I saw this guy fold up his jacket, place it on the ground and then climb up on to the parapet.

'I stopped the cab, got out and shouted at him, "What are you doing?"

'He stared at me, turned and jumped into the Thames. He surfaced and started swimming frantically as if he had changed his mind. The tide was going out and the undercurrent took him quickly across the river to the north bank in seconds. Someone rang the police but it was too late – he disappeared beneath a barge and that was the last I saw of him.

'The police found his body several weeks later upstream along the Chelsea Embankment. They told me that he had been an ex-military man, separated from his wife, who had become severely depressed and turned to heavy drinking.

'Upset by what happened, I asked myself whether, if I had grabbed him from the parapet, I might have saved him, but the police told me if I had tried he might have taken me with him down into the river.

'I have been driving a cab for twenty-two years. I'm known to my friends at the St John's Wood shelter as "B&Q".'

This is Mr Duracell.

Jeff is just finishing his tea,
and he and Steve are off to their cabs,
back into the streets of London.

'Be lucky'

probably the most
common words used
when cabbies part

In a minute of anger, the wood that has taken all year to collect is burnt.

Never try to teach your father to have babies.

If you don't know where you're coming from, then how do you know where you're going to?

Every cloud has a silver lining.

The best surprise is no surprise.

What's bred in the bone comes out in the flesh.

Love is a temporary state of madness.

A big mouth doesn't make a big man.

The more luck you give away, the more luck you have.

Walls have ears.

The harder you work, the luckier you get.

Chill out.

Another day, another dollar.

It is better to live the life of a tiger for one day than live the life of a sheep for a hundred days.

Follow that cab.

What appears to be someone's weakness could be their strength.

You will find.

If you have your health, everything else is a bonus.

He who argues with a fool is a bigger fool.

Nothing ventured, nothing gained.

Home is where the heart is.

If you are not yourself,
then you are nobody.

A man without a dream has nothing to
live for.

Beauty is in the eye of the beholder.

Good comes out of bad.

One man's meat
is another man's poison.

Luck is when preparation meets
opportunity.

A man who loves nothing fears nothing.
A man who fears nothing has no love
for life.

Yesterday was history, tomorrow is a
mystery, today is a gift.

Never run for a bus – there's always
another one around the corner.

It's not what you get from life, but what
life expects of you.

Life is a mystery to be lived.

Don't ever throw the boomerang.

Fight poverty, marry wealth.

What I like most about money is that
it doesn't clash with anything I wear.

Money is better than the mother-in-law,
as you can always get rid of it.

Flattery gets you nowhere.

Nice guys come last.

If you dig a grave for somebody,
you usually fall in it.

Life is a moment.

It's not over till the fat lady sings.

Don't teach your grandmother
how to suck eggs.

Money isn't everything, it's the only thing.

If you're bored
with London,
you're bored
with life.

So happy now

'I had a business, but my life was full of problems, so I turned to drink. People don't understand that drinking problems are not only confined to the drunk in the streets, but affect ordinary people who don't know how to handle a crisis.

'I would go home after a day's work, and hide behind a "closed door". Here with the comfort of my drink, I would escape from the reality of life without the knowledge of anyone. This went on for ten years.

'But with time you become excessive, deceitful, go into debt. You find you then affect the people around you, especially those who love you. I lost my friends and my girlfriend, and ruined my business, and this was entirely my fault.

'I was fortunate. I got help from AA (Alcoholics Anonymous). I went to a "dryout place" for six weeks, where with the help of others I put my life together. Then I came up with an idea of forming a company. When a couple of my old mates visited me I told them about it. At first they didn't trust me. Why should they? I had let down so many people. But later we formed a biotech company, floated it on the Stock Exchange and made a "pretty penny".

'I have not drunk now for five years, am back with the woman I love, got married two years ago, and am happier now than I could have ever dreamt possible.'

PADDINGTON STATION TO DRURY LANE

Something unexpected

'I am from Kampala, Uganda. I work as a lawyer, have come to London on business.

'In 1982 while I was at home with a colleague something unexpected came up, and we had to go to Masaka on some important business. I could not go at that moment so my colleague went, and I was to follow. Two hours later I got a telephone call to say that he had died in a car crash before getting to Masaka.'

QUEEN ELIZABETH CONFERENCE CENTRE TO

MOUNT ROYAL HOTEL

44

If I'd been there ten seconds earlier

'I am from Chicago, USA. I used to work in London for four years as a network manager.

'In the summer of 1996 I was going down the Strand when I heard a big bang behind me. I didn't think anything more about it. But next day I read in the newspapers that a terrorist bomb had gone off, doing serious damage. The thought of it shook me – I kept thinking it could have been me. If I had been there ten seconds earlier my life might have been a different story – I suppose that's fate.'

ROSEBERY AVENUE TO STRAND

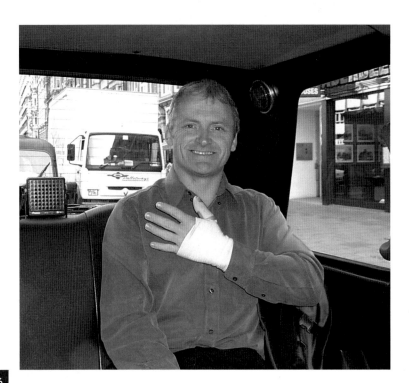

Lucky to be alive

'What's wrong with your hand?'
I asked.

'Well, I'm lucky to be here.'
He took a deep breath, sat deep in
the back seat and told me his story.

'I travel in from Coventry every
day on my motorbike. Two weeks
ago, after leaving the M40 and
going on to the A40, I'd slowed
down to about 30 mph in the
middle lane, when someone hit me
up the back, my bike caught the
car in front and I was sent flying
on to the central reservation.
The driver didn't even stop, I didn't
even see who it was, and there were
no witnesses. The ambulance
arrived and took me to Ealing
hospital. I sustained only three
fractured fingers, six fractured ribs
and if it hadn't been for my leather
gear my injuries might have been
life threatening. So you see, I'm
lucky to be alive, lucky to see
another day in my life.'

EUSTON STATION TO PRESCOT STREET

Experiencing miracles

'I am from Richmond. I've been a gynaecologist for twenty years. I love my job, being with babies, experiencing miracles every day.

'One morning a month ago, I had a bizarre experience at my clinic. I noticed in my first patient's notes that day that she had the same birthday as I did and then in my second patient's notes that she also had the same birthday as I did, and this I found all a bit too spooky. Then I was interrupted, and had to go and see a patient whom a junior doctor was having problems diagnosing. I started chatting with the patient and told her about my unusual experience that morning, and she asked me when my birthday was.

'"It's 1 December."

'"So is mine!" she replied.'

SUSSEX GARDENS TO HARLEY STREET

It was karma

'I always dreamt of becoming a successful businessman. At the age of nineteen I started working for an agency but it only lasted a month.

'Fifteen years passed. Nothing really happened till one night, on my way somewhere I decided to stop at this bar for a drink. I met an old colleague whom I hadn't seen since my first work days in my first job at a bar. It was amazing how we had met by chance. We chatted all night, realised we had a lot in common and then, when the bar closed, we continued chatting in another bar and then eventually ended up in an all-night restaurant. At 3 a.m., having spoken for seven hours and lost track of time, we decided to take a chance and start an agency.

'That was the best thing that had ever happened to me, it was karma. The agency was a success. We started with two employees, and now three years on we have over twenty people working for us.'

EUSTON STATION TO CHELSEA HARBOUR

I went along to the party

'I am from Moscow, Russia, and work here in London. I was invited by a work colleague to a high-profile party. I didn't know what to expect, but I had nothing else to do that night so I went along. I found it different to what I knew, but then just before I was going to leave I met this interesting lady. She became my friend, later my boss. She introduced me to her family including her son and like a fairytale I fell in love with him.

'We are now engaged and planning to get married.'

CHARING CROSS ROAD TO PADDINGTON STATION

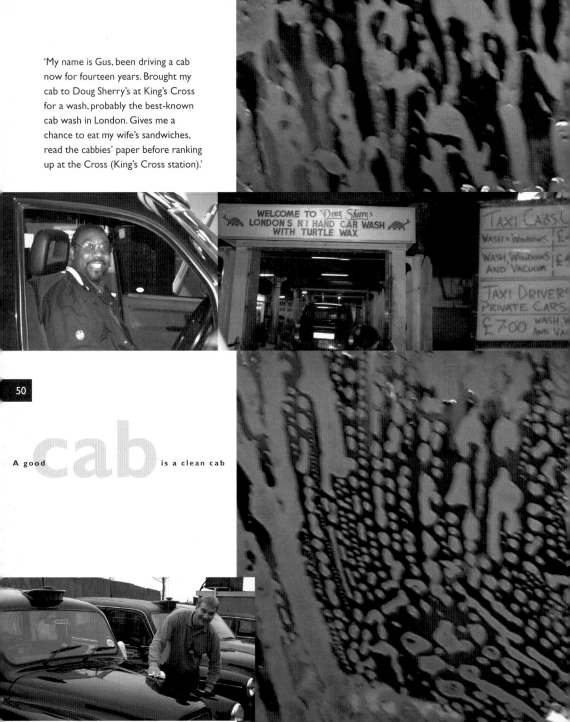

'My name is Gus, been driving a cab now for fourteen years. Brought my cab to Doug Sherry's at King's Cross for a wash, probably the best-known cab wash in London. Gives me a chance to eat my wife's sandwiches, read the cabbies' paper before ranking up at the Cross (King's Cross station).'

50

A good **cab** is a clean cab

If I had a wish

It was Saturday night when I picked up this passenger. He wanted to go to Bow Church, Bow Road.
So I switched my meter on, and headed down Jamaica Road to the Rotherhithe Tunnel. After a few minutes I broke the silence.

'Going to Bow Church – have you an appointment with God?' I asked.

'I wish ... I know what I would ask him for.' He paused for a moment, then continued, 'I have had a hard life. I used to be a bricklayer, till my knees went. Now I am unemployed, I've been divorced for twelve years and have three kids to take care of. Sometimes I find it hard, but I try my best to cope. If I had a wish I would ask him for the lottery numbers, then I'd know my kids will be OK.'

We arrived at Bow Church, he got out, paid his fare then disappeared into the night.

JAMAICA ROAD TO BOW CHURCH, BOW ROAD

People see ghosts, elves and trolls

'I am from Reykjavik, Iceland. I am a biologist and have been in London for three years. My country has lava, hot springs and in winter total darkness. People see ghosts, elves and trolls. They say that there are unbelievable shapes in the lava including trolls who turn to stone when they see the sun. Also people think that triangular mountains and glaciers are energy sources.

'We also have thirteen Father Christmases and they are wicked – they play tricks on people. Their mum, Gryla, eats children if they don't behave!'

ROSEBERY AVENUE TO CLEVELAND STREET

Four kind people in forty minutes

'I was going home on my bike when I took a bend on Buckingham Palace Road at a reckless speed, lost control and went into some railings. I found myself badly bruised, shaken and lying in a big heap on the road. A skinny black gentleman then came running over to help me, followed by another gentleman. They both helped me off the road, told me I was fortunate to be wearing a helmet and asked me if there was anything they could do since I didn't want an ambulance. I thanked them for their kindness and saw them on their way.

'I left my ruined bike tangled in the railings and went to Sloane Square tube. While waiting on the platform for the train, I noticed a crowd staring at me, and then a young girl came up and said, "Do you need any help?"

'"No, why?" I replied.

'"Because your face is covered in blood." She took out a handkerchief from her handbag and cleaned my face, while I stood baffled by a stranger's kindness. When the train arrived, I thanked her and got on to my train, where I met an old man who insisted on accompanying me till I had reached my destination.

'When I got home my wife told me off for having a second accident in three weeks. I was lucky this accident wasn't fatal, but fortunate that I met four kind people in forty minutes – now that must be a record.'

BISHOPSGATE TO ST JAMES'S PARK

Papillon

At about 10 a.m. on a Saturday morning before starting work, I stopped in Gray's Inn Road to post a letter and I noticed this man sitting on a bench, someone I had not seen around here before.

'Good morning, sir.'

'Good morning,' I replied.

Before getting back into the cab I tried to make some conversation, but all he kept saying was 'Papillon, Papillon, Papillon …' Now what was he talking about, I hadn't a clue. Anyway I gave him some fruit and bid him farewell, and that was the last I saw of him.

Then two days later, on Monday morning, I picked up my first customer from a bus stop in Shacklewell Lane.

'My grandfather died two weeks ago. I miss him. He was a sea captain, served most of his life in the royal navy. During the Second World War he escorted Russian Atlantic convoys. After the war he lived in Venezuela, Barbados and New Orleans and when he became old he came back home to the Isle of Man. He was never short of telling stories and always had a surprise for us.

'When a couple of weeks ago he passed away, the whole family gathered after the cremation to pay their last respects. I will never forget that day. As we sat in silence, the warm sun shining through the stained glass brightening the whole chapel, a beautiful butterfly appeared from nowhere, fluttering about. It touched my father on the shoulder and we found this funny, thinking it was the old sea captain's last surprise.

'Then on Friday, a day before the Grand National, I was given a tip on the Internet from someone I didn't know. He told me to put a bet on Papillon (the word is French for butterfly). I immediately thought of the butterfly I saw in the chapel, a good omen.

'So I put a £20 bet on at ten to one, and on the day of the race put on another £10, and my family put some money on. What a race it was at the 3.45 at Aintree! Yes, Papillon came first, we collected £760 and we celebrated with a toast to my grandfather, the old sea captain.'

I found this story unbelievable, so I went to the nearest newsagent and bought a copy of *The Times*. On page thirty-one, column seven, of the sports section I found the results of Saturday's 3.45 race at Aintree.

SHACKLEWELL LANE TO ISLINGTON HIGH STREET

Saturday's racing results

Aintree

Going: good, good to firm in places

1.45 1, **Sharpaten** (16-1); 2, Grimes (7-1); 3, Out On A Promise (15-2). Dee Pee Tee Cee 9-2 fav. 13 ran. NR: Silence Reigns.

2.20 1, **Jungli** (12-1); 2, Samakaan (10-11 fav); 3, Clifton Beat (7-2). 7 ran. NR: Aghawadda Gold, Flying Instructor.

2.55 1, **Mister Morose** (16-1); 2, Mantles Prince (14-1); 3, Effectual (14-1). Hors La Loi III 4-5 fav. 10 ran. NR: Master Beveled.

3.45 1, **Papillon** (10-1); 2, Mely Moss (25-1); 3, Niki Dee (25-1); 4, Brave Highlander (50-1). Dark Stranger (fell) 9-1 fav. 40 ran.

4.35 1, **Lakefield Rambler** (6-1); 2, Father Andy (14-1); 3, Finnow Thyne (16-1). Satchmo (fell) 11-4 fav. 10 ran.

5.15 1, **Quadco** (33-1); 2, Rose of Tracarta (25-1); 3, Patriarch (6-1). Inon 5-2 fav. 10 ran.

My first time in London

'I am from Dumfries, Scotland. I am now seventy-one years old and retired last year as a shop assistant.

'I have come to London with my daughter-in-law, who has an invitation for a presentation at the Dome. This is my first time in London and I am looking forward to the experience.'

EUSTON STATION TO BAKER STREET

Two English gentleman

'My name is Stan and this is Harry. We are two English gentlemen and have come down from Cheshire to have lunch at the Tower of London.'

EUSTON STATION TO TOWER HOTEL

The dentist

'I am a Londoner. I've been
a dentist for eight years.
Dentistry is a bit like getting
your books done and
submitting them to the Inland
Revenue. Nobody actually
enjoys it but it is an essential
part of life.'

WATERLOO STATION TO WIMPOLE STREET

The textile man

'I am from north Yorkshire. I work in textiles. About seven years
ago I had an encounter – I passed this woman in the street and I
felt a strong attraction to her. I went to an estate agent to buy a
house and she walks in. What a bit of luck, I thought. Apparently
she worked there.

'I wanted her to show me around this house, which I couldn't
afford. She did and I realised she was the woman of my dreams.
The following week I rang up several times, making more
enquiries about the house, but they were just an excuse to speak
to her.

'This couldn't go on, so I went to her work one day thirty
minutes before she closed and asked her out and she said yes.
'We have now been married for three years.'

VICTORIA STATION TO COMMERCIAL ROAD

The knowledge boys

I had always wanted to dance, so one night I gave it a go. I went along to Ceroc, a modern dance similar to salsa. Here in a crowded hall, people danced to the music. It was great. Among them I noticed a stunning dark-haired woman who turned, moved with a flair that stood out amongst the rest and I couldn't help but watch her in amazement for the rest of the evening. I wanted to become part of it, to one day be good enough to dance with her. So I started attending lessons, trying to learn to move my two left feet.

I went home confused by what I had experienced and was woken in the middle of the night by my window rattling. I got out of bed and went to investigate. I looked outside. The city was asleep. At the bottom of the garden, beneath the old oak tree, two lovers' silhouettes were dancing. I closed the window, went back to bed. The night was to change me for ever!

I started dancing regularly with her. Then she stopped coming and I heard her husband had died from cancer. He was only thirty-three years old. Her whole world had been devastated. She had planned to have a family with him. Now he was taken away from her and she was left in ruins.

I got chatting to a passenger …

One evening, several months later, she turned up early before any of her regular partners. This was my chance to ask her to dance. She would probably refuse for I was only a beginner, but to my surprise she accepted the dance. The DJ played a tune:

Our shadows touched,
Our souls embraced.
We danced away
To the rhythm,
To the music,
To a place
I've never seen,
Never felt before.
She took me into a dream.

I saw her again at dancing the following year: we became friends and would talk for hours on the telephone. One rainy night when she had returned to France where her parents were living, she rang me from a telephone box and broke down in tears, telling me of her pain, her grief and that she didn't know how to cope with her life. I was so moved that I decided to do something I had never done before. For the next four days I worked around the clock decorating her home, both inside and out. I moved radiators, added lights and plugs and finished it off with a bunch of yellow and blue spring flowers I put with a card in her front room.

When she returned she was shocked and so moved by what I had done that she rang her family and at that moment I saw a smile through her tears. That was the happiest day of my life.

She became my best friend based on three promises: one, that we would never flirt with anyone; two, that we would never do anything dishonest behind each other's back; and three, that if either of us ever wanted to end the relationship without any questions asked, they just had to say, 'Don't want to be your friend any more.'

We started going out in spring – we cycled through Epping and the beautiful villages of Suffolk, we travelled to Portugal and to romantic Prague. She took me to France, where she introduced me to her family and in a church in Albi I wrote a prayer for her in the visitors' book. I took her to the secluded sandy beaches of northern Cyprus where the turtles swim, then up to St Hilarion, the fairytale castle that sits high on a rocky peak.

She tried to teach me to dance with style, but because I moved like a bear she nicknamed me Baloo from The Jungle Book.

Three years passed. It was autumn, there was a wind of change – she wanted more space because of her bereavement and I agreed gladly. She started going Lindy Hop dancing. Later, she wanted to become friends again and I thought nothing of it, till one night I sensed that something was very wrong. I left a message on her machine saying,
'I know there's something you're not telling me.'

The next day she rang me. She then broke the news that she had met someone else. He was a consultant, an academic like herself, a good dancer and one of the crowd. I realised then he knew more moves than I could imagine.

The DJ had played the last tune,
The dance was over,
Lights switched on,
The dream was no more …

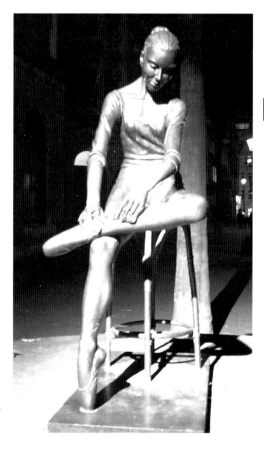

The photographer from Santa Fe

Being a cabbie is special: you can create a bond with a stranger in five minutes, talk about yourselves as if you have known each other for a lifetime and then, when they get out, you go your separate ways.

This passenger, an American photographer from Santa Fe, New Mexico, had got lost in the maze of Shoreditch's little streets full of history and intrigue (Jack the Ripper). He saw my hire light and flagged me down.

'Hi, cabbie, great to find you, I'm trying to get to the Barbican and I'm lost.'

'No problem, sir, get in, take off your shoes and make yourself at home, we aren't too far,' I said.

He was a hunk of a man, had a warm smile, and we spoke about photographic experiences.

'I got to tell you that we have a joke back home that it's impossible to find a taxi-driver who can speak English and knows where he's going,' he continued. 'Love your cab, you're professionals.'

'Thanks, sir.'

It took about twenty minutes to get there and somehow I wished it had lasted longer. I didn't

charge him for the fare. He told me he would send me his book of photos and then he took out of his pocket a coin and gave it to me.

'This coin has brought me luck,' he said. 'I would like you to have it.'

I gratefully accepted it, and then we shook hands and parted. Three weeks later I received a parcel, a special delivery from Santa Fe. It was, as promised, his book. His name was Dirk Wales.

SHOREDITCH HIGH STREET TO THE BARBICAN CENTRE, SILK STREET

The salesman

I picked up this middle-aged salesman. He said that he had been married, and spent a lot of his life driving around the country and sleeping in hotel rooms. One evening, he had met this attractive 23-year-old blonde at a hotel bar and they got chatting. He didn't believe his luck and at the end of the evening they went to bed together. For him it was the beginning of a romance.

He would see her often and spoil her with expensive gifts, and then when she asked him to divorce his wife, he did. He purchased a flat, they set up a home together and whatever she wanted he gave her. She bought herself a car on his account without asking him and soon he started getting into financial difficulties, so he worked longer hours to keep up.

Then one night she told him she had had enough, was going back to her husband.

The shock devastated him. He took to the bottle, got involved in a car crash. He found himself in the early hours of the morning in a police cell 'being given his rights'.

The duty sergeant told him that they knew about her – that she and her husband worked on the buses and when short of cash she would go in search of lonely men.

63

A day in summer

Hasn't been a morning
Haven't seen her
In my thoughts,
In my travels.
Amongst the yellow flowers
Of Covent Garden,
Amongst the shoppers
Of Oxford Street.
Pass her by,
Try to blank her
From my mind,
But thoughts of her
Are driving me crazy,
What am I to do?

I rev up,

I burn up,

Turn the cab around

In the middle of New Bond Street

To a chorus of blazing horns,

Race to reach her,

Find it isn't her.

What am I to do?

Switch off my hire light,

Go to a park.

Try to write a poem

But find myself lost

Amongst the silence of the trees,

Amongst the swans of beauty

Sliding with grace

Upon the shimmering water of a lake.

I look up to the sky

The clouds

They're drifting away,

I write, 'Sail away …'

The hand of God

'I am from New Orleans, USA. I'm here with my family for the first time. I am a religious writer, been dedicated to my profession for a long time. It began when I was nine years of age, when I asked Jesus Christ to forgive me of any sin and come and live inside my life. He saved me and now lives in my heart. That was the greatest day of my life.'

I was moved by his story. Then I did something I've never done before, I opened my folder, removed a copy of my poem 'Just One Wish', gave it to him as a gift and told him he could use it any way he liked.

At that moment his wife entered the conversation. 'Have you ever read the Gospel of St John?'

'No, but strange as it may sound, my nickname is John.'

'You must read it,' she said.

I dropped them at Buckingham Palace as the Horse Guard Parade proceeded down the Mall towards us. They got out of the cab, paid the fare, then, as they departed, his wife reiterated what she had said. 'Don't forget to read the Gospel of St John.'

I thought nothing more about it, continued work till 8 p.m., went to George's Central Fish Restaurant to have cod and chips and meet up with some cabbie friends.

LEADENHALL STREET TO BUCKINGHAM PALACE

On Monday I went back to work. It was a miserable morning, the rain catching people out as they tried to get to work through the busy streets. At about 1.15 p.m. I picked up an old man from Euston station with a Welsh accent, wanted to go to Dulwich. So we set off through the heavy traffic of Russell Square, down Southampton Row, past Holborn station and over Waterloo Bridge where the traffic filtered away. When we reached the Old Kent Road he broke the silence.

'How's your day been, son?'

'Not sure, sir,' I replied.

'Yes,' he said. 'Well, I have known my wife all my life, we were childhood sweethearts, I lived just up the road from her in Wales. Then she had a bad accident, was hit by an American truck, she was very badly hurt. I asked for God's forgiveness ...'

The old man spoke about the Bible, reminding me of the gentleman I met on Friday. He spoke about God's love, but my mind was somewhere else – I was lost in the emotions of my break-up at the weekend and my thoughts drifted away. He continued speaking as we passed through Peckham, where we encountered major roadworks, forcing me to make a major diversion.

We arrived at about 2 p.m., it was still raining and this old man had spoken with warmth throughout the journey to comfort me with my feelings.

'Sorry, I'm a bit short, only have a £20 note,' he said.

'No problem.'

'Don't forget, God is all around, he is here, in your cab.'

His words struck a chord. I shook myself out of my daze, looked at him in the eyes. Through the window he passed me the note, inside a little book. I wondered what it was.

'This is for you,' he said 'The Gospel of St John.'

EUSTON STATION TO DULWICH

The kind of experience a cabbie seldom forgets

Sometimes on a journey you meet someone, maybe just for a few minutes, and quickly you get into a conversation with them as if you have known them all your life. A bond of trust and understanding is created with a stranger. It's meetings like these that make our job special.

This passenger was one such person. He was going to visit his mother, whom he hadn't seen for a while – he wanted to see her to tell her that he loved her. He spoke of his blind stepfather who had treated him like a son, gave him so much warmth and guidance in life and would say, 'Always keep your face to the sun, the shadows will then fall behind you.' His words touched a chord.

When we got there, he invited me in to meet his mother and have some tea, but it was getting late, and I had to get back to London.

'I would like you to have this picture I've drawn for you,' he said. I accepted it, put it away in my folder.

Back in London, stuck in traffic, I looked at my gift. I was moved. I thought that if only more people were like him, this world would be a nicer place. I knew we would never meet again, but it was the kind of experience a cabbie seldom forgets.

EUSTON ROAD TO ASHTEAD, SURREY

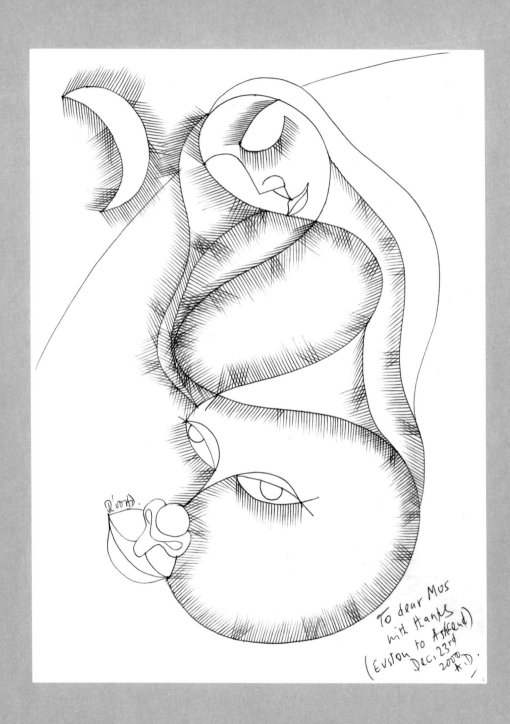

To dear Mos
with thanks
(Euston to Ashford)
Dec, 23rd
2000
K.D.

The Italian

'I like coming to London, it is a great city.
I am from Verona, Italy. It is also a great city,
where Shakespeare got his inspiration to write
Romeo and Juliet.

'Verona is an old town with a lot of history
including the old tower which is very high.
The inhabitants never go up, for it is said
to be very unlucky. There have been many
suicides over the years, especially from
foreigners who go up and view the beauty
of our city, get excited and jump off.

'Maybe this is where Shakespeare got the
inspiration
to write his play, I think.'

I asked my Italian passenger,
'Have you ever been up the tower?'

'Never,' he replied.

KENSINGTON HIGH STREET TO REGENT STREET

He shredded it

'My name is Harry and this is my guide dog, Oak, a Labrador who's seven years old. Thanks to Oak I'm mobile, he's my eyes, and thanks to him I'm able to visit my brother in Talke, Stoke-on-Trent. Oak is my best friend, but he has a bad habit of grabbing whatever he finds on the floor – an example being last week when this man dropped a fiver in the street. Before the man could pick it up, Oak grabbed it and shredded it. What could I say?'

EUSTON STATION TO VICTORIA STATION

Nice to meet you

'Where I come from you become either a football player or a pop star, or else just stay where you are.

'I used to lay down cable, hated it. Turned my anger into music and started doing gigs. One night, while doing a gig, a guy kept on rudely interrupting. I responded by pretending it was part of the act. He almost pushed me to the limit – I almost got off that stage to give him a piece of my mind. Watching all this was a person who was doing some "talent spotting". He was one of the top three in the country. He thought it was all part of the performance and was impressed. Asked me for a tape of my gigs. Now, thanks to him, I have become a success. My first album, *Northern Son*, is coming out soon and I will be performing live at Glastonbury this weekend.'

EUSTON STATION TO WESTBOURNE PARK ROAD

I could feel a presence

'I visited Newstead Abbey, near Nottingham, where Lord Byron, his mother and other famous people lived.

'After walking around the gardens and the ground floor of the abbey I went upstairs and into the bedroom where Byron's mother stayed. When I went into the room, I could feel a presence – something was trying to drive me out of the room, making me feel unwelcome. I tried to resist but I couldn't – it was all too spooky.

'I went to the bookshop, and was told that I wasn't the first person to experience something weird in the abbey, and also that Mary Shelley, the author of *Frankenstein* (1818), stayed here and she was associated with "black art".

'I recommend that you go to the abbey, cabbie – it's an experience.'

CHARING CROSS STATION TO HOLBORN CIRCUS

Meet Diesel and Tricky

One Saturday, I had just dropped off a job at Clapham Common when two gentlemen came running across the road, full of party spirit, wanted the Latchmere pub. They introduced themselves as 'Diesel' (from Manchester) and 'Tricky' (from Aberdeen). They reminded me of Morecambe and Wise, two great comedians I used to watch on television. These two guys from the moment they got in started telling me gags as if I was their audience.

I turned the cab around and headed up the Queenstown Road. I was so amused by their presence and their hilarious gags that I couldn't stop laughing. My curiosity aroused, I asked them how they met.

'You really want to know?' said Diesel.

'Please,' as I tried to stop laughing at the last joke they'd told me.

'Well, it was five years ago, March 1996 to be precise. I was a royal navy helicopter pilot then, and I got a distress call asking me to rescue some fishermen off Peterhead (near Aberdeen). It was a tricky operation, but we plucked them from the sea in gale force conditions just in time. It was all part of the job, but I got a bonus, not only saved some lives but also made a friend, gave him a nickname, 'Tricky'.'

We reached the Latchmere pub, where they got out and paid me with a tip. Tricky continued by telling me another gag with his tongue hanging out. It was hilarious – I just couldn't stop laughing. We shook hands, and they went into the pub, where I heard a loud applause of laughter from a crowd inside. What a night it was!

CLAPHAM COMMON TO LATCHMERE ROAD

You must have a strong heart

'I am from Stockholm, Sweden. I am
a maritime lawyer, and I have lived in London
for ten years. Saunas are much enjoyed
in my country. They are popular mainly
near a lake or the seashore, where after
the sauna you can either have a shower
or take a dip in the water.

'In winter after a sauna, you can roll in
the snow or better still you can drill a hole
in the ice and then jump in it – but you must
have a strong heart.'

WATERLOO STATION TO THE GUILDHALL

The lady from Texas

'I was born in Brookland, USA. I work in advertising and am here in London on business. About thirteen years ago I met the man of my life in a restaurant where we worked.
He was kind and thoughtful and made me happy. Then on Christmas Eve in his parents' living room in Vermont we were married, by his father, who is a judge.

'His mother gave us some advice that day that's become the pillar of our marriage: 'Never yell at each other unless the house is on fire.'

VICTORIA STATION TO THE ALDWYCH

The Chelsea pensioners

I was driving along the Mall on a rainy day, having decided to switch off my hire light because I needed to get to the toilet in the Strand, when I saw these two elderly 'soldier boys' flagging me down. I felt obliged to stop, so I did.

'Hope you two aren't going too far because I'm desperate to get to a loo,' I said.

'We're lost, cabbie, we're trying to get to the Union Jack Club, Sandal Street,' said one of them.

'No problem, jump in, I'll take you, I'll find another lavatory. There's no charge for this ride,' I said.

'Thanks, cabbie.' Then the pensioner continued, 'I don't know how you cabbies do it because I always seem to get lost. I recall once when I was in charge of making a delivery of fuel in the desert we lost our way, didn't have a clue where we were. After two days, having searched helplessly in the exhausting heat, we came across this British HQ group which I knew nothing about. But the commander, a brigadier, had been waiting desperately for fuel for his tanks for days. He was amazed how I found him and commended me for my map reading. So we unloaded the fuel and the Brigadier and his tanks disappeared back into the desert and so did we.'

Nice story, I thought. When we arrived at Sandal Street, they thanked me for the ride and I hastily drove on to the lavatory at the BP garage to empty myself …

THE MALL TO SANDAL STREET

It was a bonus
not to have got hurt

'During the Second World War, I served as a pilot in the RAF and I am very proud of that.

'I was a flight lieutenant then, attached to 247 Squadron Transport Command. We flew Dakota planes (tugs) and each plane towed a military glider, which carried 28–30 troops. At 2,000–4,000 feet the gliders were released.

'I was involved in the Nijmegen drop in June 1944. It was a disaster for our boys: 30 per cent of the 600 gliders sent were shot down and crashed, killing most of our troops.

'I am now seventy-eight years and as I said before am proud to have served my country.

'In those days when you got hurt you didn't go and sue – it was a bonus not to have got hurt.'

CHARING CROSS STATION TO KING'S CROSS STATION

The magic of Albert Bridge

Over the years I've heard many stories about this city, including the 'magic of Albert Bridge'. I dismissed this as myth.

Then one day I picked up an old lady who told me it was true about the bridge; it sometimes 'whispers, tells you stories'.

I decided to visit the bridge. I switched off my hire light, went down to Chelsea Embankment, parked up my cab and took a stroll beside the Thames. Here, after a sunny day, just before dusk, there was a calm feeling as everyone was going home.

I passed the Peace Pagoda until I came to the statue of the boy and the dolphin, where as if by a spell, it cast me onto Albert Bridge. I noticed something special about this place. It's difficult to explain except that it was enchanting. I couldn't help but gaze in silence upriver to the little boats bobbing on the water, shimmering like stars in the night. The sun absorbed me in beautiful light, took me away into fantasy…

The view from Albert Bridge

bridge, Gem's father had an accident, fell to his death into the ravine. Gem's mother had died when he was born. Now he had nothing left except for a little cabin, his father's axe and the bridge they built together. Two years passed. It was the month of spring; trees were blossoming in yellows and pinks, squirrels played and butterflies danced and alpine scents covered the mountains. Gem was on the bridge that morning, singing one of his father's songs, when he heard the sound of horses approaching. He turned to see a carriage drawn by three horses slowing down almost to a trot as it passed. He glanced at the carriage, saw a beautiful woman wearing a yellow ribbon around her long black hair. She had a twinkle in her eyes, gave Gem a blushing smile.

'Who are you?' Gem asked, but he got no reply. The carriage picked up speed as it left the bridge, entering the kingdom and disappearing into the Greenwood Forest.

Gem felt warmth, a buzz inside like he had never felt before. Was this love? Was it a dream? He did not know the answer. In desperation he searched the kingdom, but could not find her.

Each morning he would go down to the bridge, wait for her, but she never came. Then, when night came, he returned to the mountains, closed himself in behind the doors of his cabin and sat in darkness, not knowing what to do. He felt a sadness, a pain deep in his soul; he longed to find her, to see her just one more time.

One warm winter's evening when the stars covered the ceiling of the universe, Gem looked out of his cabin window and saw a shooting star whizzing across the dark skies. He searched

1 I imagined that in this place long ago, before the days of Robin Hood and of the Knights of the Round Table, there was once a small kingdom called Camelot. It was inaccessible from the mountains and from the high seas. There was only one way in and that was across a wooden bridge, which stretched across a deep ravine that separated the kingdom from the outside world.

Albert, the woodsman of the kingdom, and his son, Gem, built the bridge. On completion of the within the pain of his soul and from his pain he found a poem. As he recited the poem he watched the shooting star burst into colours such as he had never seen before.

His friends were concerned that they had not seen him for a while and visited him to find out what was wrong. Gem replied by reciting them the poem. They listened, they cried, they applauded. When they left, they forgot the words. People heard about Gem's poem and came from all around to sit beside the cabin fire and listen to it. There were those who came who tried to steal his words either by writing them down, or simply by memorising them, but when they left the cabin the poem disappeared into thin air.

What they did not know was that those words were magic. They did not realise that you cannot steal what comes from the soul.

2 King Alfred of Camelot was an old man whose only love in life was for his daughter, Eleanor. Her mother, the Queen, had died when giving birth to her. On the day of her birth two exotic birds appeared in the palace. They never sang, never left the Princess's side. As the Princess grew in beauty, the King feared that he would lose the only thing he loved in life, so her face was always hidden from the subjects of the kingdom. For this reason the Princess spent most of her day confined to the palace gardens with her birds. Here, amongst the flowers and their colours, she sang to them about the dreams she had.

One summer's day she fell down some steps in the palace gardens and hit her head upon a pillar. She went into a deep coma. She was carried to her chamber and the physician told the King that she would die unless she could be brought out of this deep sleep. The physician tried everything he knew but nothing worked. The King announced that whoever could save the life of the Princess would be rewarded with whatever they wished. So they came from far, from near, to seek their fortune. From behind a screen in the Princess's chamber, they tried everything imaginable, but still nothing worked. The Princess was sinking deeper into sleep, deeper towards death. The physician had exhausted his ideas – he didn't know what to do. Then in the corridors of the palace a rumour spread: 'What about the woodsman with the magic poem?' The physician heard, and so did the King. Gem was asked to come at full speed, so he did.

Behind the screens he was left alone. Behind

the screens he searched into his heart. Amongst his pain, amongst his tears, he found his poem. He recited the words:

Take my hand
And I will take
You
Across the seas.
Take my hand
And I will take
You
Across the skies.
Take my hand
And I will take
You
To the
Never Never Land
Where the White Mountains
Touch the clouds.
There under the
Moonlight
We could wine,
We could dine,
We could dance,
Till the awakening of the
Dawn.
Take my hand
And if you like
I will be your
Friend
Till the end
Of time.

Gem wiped a tear from his cheek, turned and solemnly walked out of the chamber, walked past the guards at the end of the corridor. Then from the silence of the palace came a scream of joy from the Princess's chamber. The Princess was awake, she was alive.

The Princess had been saved. The guards danced with joy, the palace burst into happiness. The King could not thank Gem enough. He offered Gem whatever his heart desired.

Gem simply asked, 'Does the Princess wear a ribbon?'

'Yes,' replied the King.

'Is it a yellow ribbon?'

'Yes,' replied the King.

'Could I please have it?'

'Yes, but why?' replied the King.

Gem never gave the King an answer. The King gave him the yellow ribbon. He tied it to his belt, turned and quietly walked from the palace, back to his cabin up in the hills.

Gem could not tell anyone about his feelings, for who has ever heard of a woodsman falling in love with a princess?

He went back to the woods to cut down trees, back to the life he had had before he met the Princess. When the sun had set in the evening sky he would go to his cabin, sit beside the fireplace without a fire and fall asleep in the darkness. He would see no one. Talk to no one. All he had in life was his cabin, his axe, memories of his father and the yellow ribbon.

3 Beyond the bridge lived a tyrant who was master of an empire that he ruled with ruthlessness. He conquered all who opposed him. He heard about the Princess's beauty. He sent messengers to ask the King for his daughter's hand in marriage. When the King refused, the tyrant fumed with anger. 'Who dares oppose me will be destroyed,' the tyrant said in rage.

Months passed, autumn came along, and the trees of the forests were of browns, bright oranges and yellows. The butterflies, the squirrels and the flowers had all gone to sleep, for the coldness of winter was on its way.

One morning, Gem had awoken late and was standing looking down the hill from the mantle of his cabin, across the bridge into the valley beyond to watch the sun rise, when he noticed a large cloud of smoke coming towards the bridge. 'What can that be?' he asked himself. Then he realised that it was horsemen, maybe three hundred in number. They were the tyrant's. Gem grabbed his father's axe from above the door and ran down the hill as fast as his legs could carry him. There was no time to lose.

On the bridge he found the two sentries sleeping. He awoke them, told them the kingdom was in danger and that they must ride to the palace to get help. This was the only chance left for the kingdom, Gem told them. Reluctantly they mounted their horses hastily and galloped off. Gem was now alone. He knew that the King would arrive too late.

Gem looked at the bridge, thought of his father, and knew then what had to be done. As the horsemen were getting closer, he ran on to the bridge halfway.

Gem raised his axe above his head, and then brought it down with all his strength. The blade cut deep into the timber of the bridge. Each time he did so he could feel the pain of his father's memories go through him, deeper and deeper.

'What is worth living for is worth dying for,' Gem yelled out as he swung the axe again and again. The horsemen were almost on the bridge. Gem knew he was almost there.

The tyrant saw what was happening as he led his horsemen on to the bridge. He quickly drew an arrow from his pouch and fired it at Gem. But it was too late.

As the horsemen were almost upon Gem half the bridge collapsed, sending the tyrant and many horsemen down into the ravine to their deaths.

4 When the King arrived with his knights, what was left of the enemy fled. The kingdom was saved, the Princess was safe, but where was Gem? They found his body upon the remnants of the bridge, with an arrow in his chest. The King tried in vain to remove it but it was too late. Gem was dead. Day became night, but the moon would not awake. They carried Gem on the shields of the knights. Folks came into the streets, and with lit candles lined the route towards the palace. The night remained silent except for the sounds of the horses' hooves and the knights' armour. They followed his body into the palace.

The Princess was in her chamber looking down from her balcony on to the square below when she saw the woodsman's body. At first she didn't recognise him; then she saw the yellow ribbon tied to his belt. Everything became clear to her. She remembered that it was him whom she had seen on the bridge, he was the one who saved her life, and he was the one she dreamed of in the palace gardens.

The Princess could take no more. She ran into the palace square. Everyone dropped to their knees, lowered their heads.

There was complete silence. She knelt beside his body, searched into the pain of her soul. Found a poem. She whispered the words into his ears:

'Take my hand
And I will take you
Across the seas …'

She started crying, then the King cried, and then everyone cried. The Princess's tears dropped upon his chest. She rose upon her feet, turned and solemnly walked towards the steps of her chamber. She stopped and turned to Gem to find that he had opened his eyes, he was alive.

Then there was a beautiful sound – it was the two paradise birds, who had never sung before. The sun came out, the people danced. There was laughter, there was joy.

The King knighted Gem and gave him the hand of his daughter in marriage. They married on the third day.

The morning after the wedding, while they slept in each other's arms in the cosiness of their bedroom,

The birds flew away
With the ribbon.
They flew three times
Around
The palace
As the sun began
To rise.
They flew from the
Kingdom of Camelot.
They flew
Across the seas,
They flew
Across the skies,
They flew to the
Never Never Land,
Where the
White Mountains
Touch the clouds,
The land
That was paradise …

To me, the characters of this
fairytale are real – I see them each
day in the streets of London.

King Alfred, known for wisdom,
stands in Trinity Square.

The tyrant, the Lord of Darkness,
stands in defiance at the entrance
to the London Dungeons.

Gem, to me, represents Richard the
Lionheart, defender of our nation,
symbol of our liberty, who stands
outside the Houses of Parliament.

The physician, known for
his loyalty to the King, stands
in Sloane Square.

Princess Eleanor, known for her
beauty and kindness, stands on
Holborn Viaduct and her monument
stands outside Charing Cross station.

The birds of paradise are to be
found on the Queen Mother's Gate
at Hyde Park.

And then there is Albert Bridge.
Take this journey at dusk and see
what you may find …

Fined ten shillings and sixpence

'I am a Londoner. My family back over four generations come from Battersea.

'In 1902 my grandfather, then six or seven years of age, was caught playing football in Battersea Park, and fined 2s. 6d. (two shillings and six pence) plus a further 2s. 6d. for playing on a Sunday. This was a lot of money to pay those days, especially for a low-income-earning family.'

EUSTON STATION TO DEVONSHIRE SQUARE

A 'nice job'

Visit us some time?

'I am from Perth, Australia, visiting London for the first time.

'Perth is in western Australia. It's probably the most isolated city in the world, has a lot of sunshine with temperatures reaching 40°C in summer, a great outdoor life. If you like to have "bush cuisine" (kangaroo, crocodile and emu) you will find it there.

'Two years ago an English family decided to immigrate to Perth and moved in next door. Then six months ago they went to visit a coastal place called Albany. Before they went I warned them of the dangers of the cliffs, slippery rocks and the reputed "king waves", which have resulted in fishermen being washed away. What was unusual was that their fourteen-year-old daughter got bitten on the leg by a shark. Now there's more chances of winning the lottery.

'Visit us some time?'

VICTORIA STATION TO PICCADILLY

Earls Court to Olympia

'A lady
wants
a cab.'

'Nice to
find a
cabbie.'

'I'm late
again – can
you try to
get me there
quickly?'

'Thanks,
cabbie,
keep the
change.'

Now isn't that amazing?

'I am an Englishman, left here twenty-five years ago for the Far East. The last ten years I have spent in Japan. I have a business there and now am happily married to a Japanese lady.

'Japan is an interesting place, full of unusual customs. For example, I once invited my staff for a drink, and as we socialised one of my male employees got emotional and told me he hated me more than anyone in the world. I was embarrassed by this incident but was later told that over a drink the Japanese could say whatever they liked without giving offence, something I found hard to stomach.

'The next evening after work, however, I invited the man to a bar, he accepted and over a drink I queried his remark of the previous night. He told me that for some reason he had always hated his employers and his remark wasn't personal.

'This chat helped relax the situation at work – in fact it improved matters and after a couple of days all was forgotten. Now isn't that amazing?'

WEST END TO KENSINGTON CHURCH STREET

On a summer's morning

It's nice when you meet someone who greets you with a smile – it makes all the difference to your day, as this lady did mine when she got into my cab in Holland Park Avenue on a summer's morning.

I couldn't resist asking her a question. 'Were you born with a smile?'

'My parents say I was.'

I continued, 'Is your name Sandra?'

'Now that's bizarre, it's my mother's name and we're very alike. Her birthday is a day after mine.'

HOLLAND PARK AVENUE TO BERKELEY SQUARE

I used to drive a sixteen-ton lorry

'I used to drive a sixteen-ton lorry for a couple of years. It was great fun. I remember once I picked up this load of road tarmac from Southampton and set off in the early hours of morning to drop it off in Oxford Street, London.

'It was the time when we had the London bombing, so it was of no surprise to find a police checkpoint. But since I had left my load unattended overnight they insisted on accompanying me to my destination. When we got there the police told me to leave the vehicle for a few hours. Now how many girls can leave their vehicles in Oxford Street and go shopping?'

PADDINGTON STATION TO NOBLE STREET

How did you know that?

Picked up this young lady from King's Cross station. She got into the cab, gave me her destination, then I said, 'You are in the armed forces.'

'How did you know that? There isn't anything with me to show that I am.'

KING'S CROSS STATION TO WATERLOO STATION

This gentleman hailed me for a cab. I stopped, opened my window and then, before he could say a word, said, 'Paddington station, sir?'

'Blimey,' he replied, 'how did you know that? Are you psychic?'

REGENT STREET TO PADDINGTON STATION

Picked up this passenger from
Buckingham Palace Road.

'Regent Street as quickly as you can,
I have an exam at 2 p.m.'

'Yes, in psychology,' I said.

'How did you know?'

BUCKINGHAM PALACE ROAD TO UPPER REGENT STREET

THE COLLEGE OF PSYCHIC STUDIES
16 QUEENSBERRY PLACE, LONDON SW7 2EB
TEL: 0171-589 3292/3

FULL MEMBER

Membership No: H.5764

Valid until: 1/10/2000

Name:

Signature:

He started yelling

'I was driving along, and stopped in a petrol station to get some petrol. After filling up, I pulled over to wait for my fella, when the car cut out. Then a man pulled into the station flashing his lights and beeping his horn. I got out to tell him the car wouldn't start, but he started yelling, "Get away from your f***ing car."

'When I looked at the car, I saw that it was on fire underneath and under the bonnet. Luckily the garage gave me some fire extinguishers to stop the garage going up in flames too. The garage was closed for twenty-four hours, they charged me for the fire extinguishers and I lost my car. I forgot that my MOT had run out on the car and I had to pay the garage fees of £200.'

EUSTON STATION TO CANARY WHARF

The songwriter

'I am a songwriter. People often ask me,
"How do you come to get a good title?"
I tell them I get a good title from anywhere.

'I had a secretary in Switzerland, she used
her home as an office. One morning I went
to her office and found her sobbing at her desk.

"What's wrong, Roxanne?" I asked.

"It's my boyfriend, Patrick, he's so cruel
to me that I told him, 'You won't find another
fool like me.'"

'These words gave me the title of a song
that became a number one hit in 1974,
sung by the New Seekers. So you see a title
is the seed of a song.'

EUSTON STATION TO THE SAVOY HOTEL

The Four Chapters

CHAPTER 1

I remember when I was a young boy my grandfather always carried this old small tin box in his jacket pocket. I would sometimes see him opening it discretely in the corner of the room when nobody was around. No one knew what was inside; it was his secret.

Then one day I had an accident and cut my knee in the school playground. I came home crying. My grandfather tried to comfort me, then he did something he had never done before. He put me on his lap and whispered in my ear, 'If you stop crying I will let you have a look in the tinderbox, but only if you promise me you will tell no one what you see.'

I nodded and pulled back my tears. He slowly put his hand into his pocket, pulled out the tinderbox. It was small and silver in colour with knocks on the edges. Again he whispered into my ear, 'Promise me, son, tell no one.'

I nodded excitedly. I held my breath. He opened the lid and just as quickly he closed it. He gave me a smile, put the tinderbox back into his pocket and left the room. I never saw him with it again.

I grow up, become a man and have this weird dream. I wrote down what I saw…

CHAPTER 2

I was clearing my grandfather's
Cellar out
A year since he passed away,
When I came
Across this tinderbox
That was secretly hidden away.

Like a cat I was curious,
Decided to open it,
When I did,
Mama mia,
Got a surprise.
Out like a flash
Came a spectrum of spiralling light.
It encircled me,
Engulfed me,
Then took me inside.
Into a world of fantasy,
Into Arabian Nights.
I found myself outside the walls
Of a deserted fortress city.
Pushed open the wooden gates,
Entered into a maze of alleyways.
What was this place?
Was it a place of magic,
Or
A place of dreams?
If so, could I find Aladdin's lamp?
Make that wish
Become rich?
But I couldn't find
A soul
To tell me which way to go.

Came to a white mosque
In a corner of a small square,
Saw a beautiful woman
With raven hair,

Walked past me
As if I wasn't there.
Who was she?
I turned,
I called
But she melted
With her shadow
Into the darkness of an alleyway…

CHAPTER 3

Three years later I picked up two passengers
from Heathrow Airport, a young woman with
her mother.

I found them charming and soon got chatting.
The daughter who was in her late twenties was shy
in nature, petite with a deep golden tan and dark-
black hair. She talked of her home in Istanbul and
had come to London to visit her sister who was
studying in Richmond. When we parted I left my
number in case they ever needed me and never
thought I would hear from them again.

The next night I got a phone call. They had been
robbed in Bayswater. I got into my cab, got to
Lancaster Gate as fast as I could and tried to
comfort them. I insisted they were my guests for
the next couple of days and they accepted. I gave
them a tour of London and a meal at Kenwood
House. We became friends, something I never
expected. When I took them back to the airport
they were so moved by a cabbie's hospitality that
they invited me to Istanbul. Later that year, in
winter, I took them up on their invitation.

CHAPTER 4

A cab took me from the airport, after a forty-
minute drive we entered through the gates into
the old walled city of Istanbul where I was to stay.

The first day the mother and daughter took me to
a restaurant along the waters of the Bosporus
where I savoured some of the delicious local fish.

Then next morning, the daughter came to the
hotel alone, took me by taxi to see the priceless
gems of Topkapi Palace, but the Palace was closed.
So instead we went to the ancient Grand Bazaar.

Here I followed her through the countless small but
noisy streets past stalls and shops selling treasures of
every kind. We somehow got lost, then something
strange came over me. I was sure I had been to this
place before. But how could I have been? I had
never been to Istanbul before. I was confused.

We arrived at an opening, a mosque in a square,
didn't believe what I was seeing, the words dawned
on me:

Came to a white mosque
In a corner of a small square,
Saw a beautiful woman
With raven hair.

The tinderbox, I thought.
'What is the name of the mosque?' I asked.
'The White Mosque,' she replied.
This is impossible, I thought. There must be an
explanation.

Nearby, next to an alleyway, I noticed a little shop,
covered in bill-posters, with a padlock and grill
over the door. It must have been closed for a long
time, I thought. Above the door, engraved in the
weathered sandstone was the word, 'Elif', the
name of my dark-haired guide.

● 'Met this man who worked the docks in Liverpool (Canada Docks) for over twenty-eight years.

'He told me there was this large barrel that smelt of rum that nobody had collected. So the dockers thought it would be a good idea to plug the barrel. They tapped it and for two years they feasted on the rum.

'When the tap went dry they decided to open the barrel to scoop out the last few drops and to their surprise they found the body of a gorilla inside.'

● 'I once had this passenger who told me, "I went to a kennel to buy a Labrador pup. I got into a row with this woman who wanted the same dog. The kennel owner came over to us and told us to leave or sort it out over a cup of tea. So we did, I asked her out for a date and she accepted. We are now married and our dog has just had pups."'

● 'I remember once I had this woman who told me she had been running to catch the five o'clock train at Charing Cross when she fell over this man's case and grazed her knee. Having missed her train she was angry, he apologised and insisted on buying her a coffee and they have been together ever since.'

● 'Dave smashed his car into Shirley's car, writing it off. Shirley made him take her to his parents' house to get the insurance details.

'Ten years later when Shirley was the boss at a company, she recognised his name and they have been with each other ever since.'

● 'I once dropped a customer off at the Savoy Hotel (Savoy Court), told him it's the only place in the UK where you drive on the right legally.

'"Well, you haven't seen my wife drive then ..." he replied.'

● 'I had this old man once, he told me he went to the food hall at Harrods, asked for an elephant sandwich. The young girl from behind the counter replied, "Sorry, sir, but we have run out of bread."'

● 'I picked up a man with a large television. He insisted on carrying it in the back of the cab. "No problem," I said.

'I took him to Tottenham Court Road as requested and he moaned the whole way about his wife making him return this television to the shop where he bought it when he could have been with his mates in the pub. When we got there, he got out, slammed the door angrily behind him. The fare was £4.20 but he shoved a £50 note at me, which I couldn't change.

'"Unlucky," he said. "Will pay you another time," and then he walked off.

'I don't believe it, I thought. I didn't want an argument, so I was driving off, when I heard this big bang. I looked in my mirror, saw him jumping up, yelling, his hands in the air. I stopped the cab, he must have found some change I thought, but he had caught the television lead in my door.'

● 'I met this man whose friend went to India on New Year's Eve. There, on a beach amongst thousands of Indians celebrating, he decided to be alone. So he took a walk up a cliff and found a temple on the top, where he met a woman. She is now his wife.'

● 'I had this man who told me he was once desperate to go to a toilet, but had no choice but to use a ladies' toilet.

'Unfortunately he was caught by an old lady, who challenged him, "Sir, this is exclusive for the ladies."

'"So is this, madam, but it occasionally has to pass water …"'

● 'I had stopped outside Friern Barnet Mental Hospital to check an address when a man peered over the wall, asked me if I could get him some cigarettes since he was not allowed out.

'Thought nothing of it, got out of my cab, got the cigarettes, returned and gave them to him. He turned and walked off back towards the hospital.

'"Wait, you haven't paid me yet."

'"What do you think I am, mad?" he replied.'

**Money cannot bring happiness,
but it sure can make being miserable
more enjoyable.**

Tell the truth and shame the devil.

The hunt is better than the kill.

The open hand has the strongest grasp.

**A bamboo that doesn't bend
in the wind breaks.**

A bird in the hand is worth two
in the bush.

**You don't grow old, you grow
and when you stop growing you get old.**

No brains, no headaches.

Never sleep on an argument.

One satisfied desire creates another.

Read between the lines.

You can lead a horse to water
but you can't make it drink.

Treat 'em mean, keep 'em keen.

If 'and' and 'but' were candy and nuts,
we would have a merry Xmas.

**If wishes were horses,
then beggars would fly.**

Your bank manager gives you
an umbrella when it's sunny, and takes
it back when it rains.

Every picture tells a story.

Today is the tomorrow of yesterday.

**Doesn't matter what you are, it only
matters what people think you are.**

What doesn't kill you
makes you stronger.

You are as old as the person you feel.

If you have nothing nice to say,
say nothing at all.

**Opportunities are never lost,
they just go to someone else.**

If you are not on the board,
you are not in the game.

What comes around goes around.

If it ain't broke, don't fix it.

QUESTION: **What is a clever man?**
ANSWER: **A clever man is a man who can make more money than his wife can spend.**
QUESTION: **What is a clever woman?**
ANSWER: **A clever woman is a woman who finds such a man.**

It is better to have loved and lost than never to have loved at all.

There's no smoke without fire.

An old man is a young man with experience.

There's many a slip 'twixt cup and lip.

The tragedy of being old is not that one is old, but that one is young.

Play the hand you're dealt.

You can shear a sheep many times, but you can only skin it once.

Winning is not the only thing, it's everything.

No sense, no feelings.

Marriage is like eating mushrooms – you don't know until afterwards if they are toadstools.

A stitch in time saves nine.

Thought before action, if you've got time.

The exception proves the rule.

If you look around the table and cannot see who the mug is, then it's got to be you.

Tomadachi

I picked up a Japanese gentleman from London Heathrow airport, Terminal 4. Our destination was the Forum Hotel, Cromwell Road. He looked jetlagged – not surprising, I thought, after an eighteen-hour flight. My customer, a well-dressed man in his mid-thirties, was here for the first time. He worked for a Japanese bank and I thought it good PR if I could say a few words in Japanese that I had picked up over the years.

'*Ohio, kon'nichiwa,*' I said (good morning friend, how are you?).

'*Asso,*' he replied, with surprise on his face, but unfortunately by the time we got on to the M4 he had fallen asleep. I drove as smoothly as possible all the way so I would not wake him up, but when we arrived at the hotel the doorman abruptly swung the door open, causing my passenger to wake up with a fright. The porter took his luggage, and the customer paid me the fare of £28.60 plus a £3 tip.

'*Dormo harygato tomadachi,*' I said (thank you, friend).

He smiled, said, '*Sayonara*' (goodbye), and walked into the hotel.

I put my hire light on and went in search of my next job. When I got to Kensington High Street a lady with shopping bags was waiting for a cab. She flagged me down and I stopped, she asked to go to Queens Park and I accepted.

Then I heard a scream. Leaving my door open, she walked off yelling, 'I'm not getting in your cab, there's something dead in the back seat.'

I looked around, and found she wasn't joking, there was something very dead. It was a black hairy object. I poked it with my crooklock, but it didn't move. I poked it again, and this time tossed it over.

Blimey, I thought, it's a wig. What am I going to do with this? I realised what an unbelievable scenario I was in. Could I imagine handing it in to lost property? They wouldn't stop laughing. But this was serious, someone out there had lost their hair, how would they be able to use their ID?

Yes, I thought to myself, it must have been my last customer, 'Tomadachi', the Japanese gentleman. The wig must have come off while he was having a nap in my cab. I wasted no time, put the wig in a carrier bag and went to the hotel, where I asked the concierge to contact the Japanese gentleman whom I just dropped off from the airport. She was a little woman who had a defiant look about her, and I knew I would have a problem with her.

'Why?' she demanded.

'Well, I've got something in this bag that I believe belongs to him,' I said, hoping she would not ask what.

'What is it?' she says.

Oh no, I thought. 'Sorry, I cannot tell.'

'In that case don't waste my time here.' Then she turned, walked off.

I had no choice but to raise my voice. 'I will therefore take your name, madam, and I will hold you directly responsible.'

She turned around, in astonishment, gave me a grumpy look, and made that call.

Ten minutes later, my passenger arrived. He looked tired, puzzled and, as I had guessed, as bald as a coot. With the bag in one hand, stroking my head with the other, I greeted him for the second time and got straight to the point.

'*Tomadachi*, have you forgotten something in my cab?'

'No,' he said.

'Have you forgotten a camera?' I said, still stroking my head, hoping he got the message.

'No, why?' he said, appearing more puzzled than ever. Then he put his right hand on his head, went red as a beetroot and yelled out something long in Japanese. I took him by the arm, showing him what I had in the bag. 'Tomadachi' gave me a sigh of relief, took the bag and shoved a fiver in my hand.

'*Durmo harygato, sayonara,*' he said with a smile (thanks, goodbye). He turned around, whistled happily and walked off, swinging the bag.

A job worth doing, I thought to myself. As I left, the woman behind the desk looked curious, changed her tune, stopped me, asked politely, 'What was all that about? What was in the bag?' she asked.

'Now that will be telling, wouldn't it …'

HEATHROW AIRPORT TO THE FORUM HOTEL

A twenty and a five

It was 10 a.m. on a busy Friday morning.
I needed a lavatory and some breakfast,
so I switched off my hire light and headed down
Rosebery Avenue to the Granby Grill. The lights
at the junction of Tysoe Street turned red,
forcing me to brake hard. While I was waiting
anxiously for them to change, a young woman in
her late teens came running from across the road.

'Greenwich, driver, as quickly as you can.'

'Sorry, love, I'm not for hire.'

'Please help me, I haven't been home all night.'

I felt sorry for her, and forgot I needed a lavatory,
but I had a bad feeling about this job. Even so,
I accepted the ride. Almost from the start I
encountered heavy traffic, something that is a fact
of life these days and there isn't much we cabbies
can do. I used all my knowledge but the traffic
was gridlocked around the city. With her
permission I took a diversion, and headed towards
Shoreditch, down Commercial Street, around
Aldgate and on to Commercial Road. I praised
myself for making a good move, leaving the chaos
behind, but this did not help my desperation for a
lavatory. After exiting the Rotherhithe Tunnel,
I noticed my passenger yawning.

'Had a late night?'

'Yes, went clubbing all night in Islington.
Paid £4.50 for these drinks and that's
expensive,' she said.

'What do you work as?' I asked.

'I don't, I'm unemployed.'

At that moment I realised that my gut feeling
was right. I could see what was coming next.

After a long pause she continued. 'I do this ride
several times a week, pay about £13.00. I won't
give you a penny more.'

I immediately replied, 'There is no way you can
get by cab from Islington to Greenwich for
£13.00, also I am not in control over the traffic.
The quicker I can get you to your destination,
the sooner I can find a lavatory.'

'If you didn't want to take me in the first place,
then why did you accept the ride?'

Now I knew her game, no way was I going to
lose my temper. She definitely had tried this
trick on cabbies before and I could have taken
her to the nearest police station, but all I wanted
now was to find a lavatory and this she knew.
When we arrived at Greenwich there was
£21.20 on the clock.

'Stop here,' she said in a cold, calculated voice.

I pulled up beside the *Cutty Sark* and she got
out of my cab. She peered through my nearside
window in an aggressive manner.

'Now the most I have ever paid for this ride is
£15.00. I won't give you a penny more.'

She shoved two notes into my hand before
walking off.

A twenty and a five.

TYSOE STREET TO GREENWICH

A cabbie picks up an Irishman three o'clock in the morning in Berkeley Square, who gives him an address on a bit of paper.

'Do you know this address?' the Irishman asks.

'Yes, it's off the Harrow Road.'

'Take me there,' he replies.

When they get there the cabbie shows him the house. 'I want you to wait for me, I won't be a minute, then take me back. Leave your door open, engine running.'

He goes to the house, rings the bell, a little guy opens the door, he headbutts him, guy collapses. He gets back into the cab and the cabbie drives off.

'What's that all about?' the cabbie demands.

'I was given this address, told he's been having a fling with my wife. Now he won't be doing that again.'

Then it dawns on the cabbie as he turns left back into Harrow Road that he has taken him to the wrong street.

Every cabbie has a story

A cabbie picks up a blonde, 2 a.m. Saturday morning, from the Sugar Club. She's dressed like a model in a low-cut dress. She asks him to take her over Chelsea Bridge to a mansion in Prince of Wales Drive. He has £8.80 on the clock.

'Sorry, but I cannot pay you.'

'What?' the cabbie replies.

'But I will make you an offer you cannot refuse – will swap you a ride for a ride!'

One night this cabbie goes to get a McDonald's in King's Cross, when a brass comes up to him, asks, 'Are you looking for business?'

'No,' replies the cabbie, 'I'm looking for a cheeseburger!'

I'm always late

'I am a Catholic girl from Ireland. I'm always late. I was meant to have been born on 4 July, American Independence Day, but was born eight days later on Orange Day – not good. In my life I've been late for most things, even if I've left early to catch a train.

'The other day my boss gave me the company car to go to a managerial training course in Borehamwood. It was the first time I had ever used a motorway. "No problem," he said.

'I got on the motorway, saw three guys waving at me from a van, lost concentration, changed lanes, took the wrong exit and got lost. Someone at work tried giving me directions over the mobile and eventually after going round a roundabout three times I finally got the right exit, and reached the course an hour and a half late.

'And then on my return, two minutes away from my work I had a car accident – now that was bad luck.'

LIVERPOOL STREET STATION TO THE STRAND

Had great fun, went piranha fishing

'I am an Australian. I work in London. I was on holiday this year in Brazil, went piranha fishing in the Pamtonaz wetlands, that is a huge lake that borders Bolivia, Peru and Brazil. I had great fun, piranha fishing in water waist high, and as long as you didn't have any cuts you were OK. If you did, they'd nip you. Anyway, it was an experience, but I only caught four piranhas all morning and they tasted disgusting.'

ALDERSGATE STREET TO MOORGATE

Every cabbie has a story

I picked up this lady who had emigrated to Australia with her seven-year-old daughter after she had got divorced.

Three years later, she was awoken one night by these bright lights whizzing across her ceiling. After several minutes they faded away and she thought nothing more about it.

The next morning she received an unexpected call from an old friend in London. She broke the news that her ex-husband had died during the night.

I was waiting on the Liverpool Street station rank, on a Thursday morning at 9.30 a.m., when this African lady comes up to me, asks for Liverpool Street.

"'This is it,'" I replied.

"'But I cannot find this place,'" she said. She gives me this map, I look at it then realise something isn't right. The streets and places are different. Then I notice the words "Liverpool FC". Oh no, I thought.

"'You have come to the wrong place. This is Liverpool Street in London, you need the city of Liverpool,'" I said.

"'Can you get me there by 10 a.m.?'"

"'You must be joking, love, it's halfway up the country,'" I replied.'

Dennis Clarke

'I picked up a nurse from Waterloo station who worked in a kidney transplant clinic. Our destination was the Stamford Hospital in Chiswick. We got chatting and the first thing I noticed was that she was a caring, warm person who had dedicated the last fifteen years to those in need.

'I remember a patient I was taking care of three and a half years ago, an old man, always dressed up. I got to know him and he told me about his life, the war, how he was captured by the Japanese and badly beaten up. Then, after the war, he looked after his sick wife till she died. Now he had nobody. I got to know and became fond of him. Then he got cancer, was transferred to a cancer hospital, knew his days were numbered. I felt a sorrow for him, but just had to get on with my job.

'Six months passed. I received a telephone call from a solicitor who had traced me to inform me that the old man had died and left me money in his will. I was given £10,000, some of which I gave to the doctors and nurses at the clinic.

'After a week the solicitor rang me again, and told me that more accounts for the old man had been discovered, so I received more money. It soon became evident that the more money I gave away, the more I received. After giving some of it to my sister for her central heating, I received a cheque for £800 from my insurance company for a wrong payment.

'This went on for a year, till one night before my wedding I had a dream of the old man. He had come to tell me, "There's no money left." He was right – I never heard from the solicitor again nor received any unexpected cheques. I visited his grave, paid my respects. His name was Dennis Clarke.'

WATERLOO STATION TO STAMFORD HOSPITAL

A short **nap** works wonders

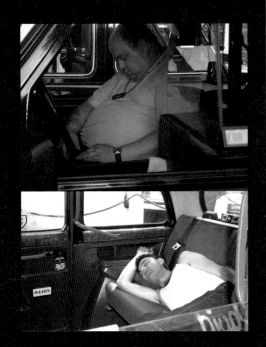

'We are from Northampton, England.'

'We are from Bergen, visiting our friend here [left] in London.'

'I have just returned from the Caribbean where I was born. I have brought back a lot of native spices so that I can enjoy my food as if I was still at home.'

Please help us

'We're from Denmark, late for an interview
at 1 p.m. Please help us – we need Worship Street.'

I looked at my watch: twenty-five minutes,
I thought. 'Will try my best,' I said to the couple.

Meter on, pedal flat down, on to the Marylebone
Road, past the long queues at Madame Tussaud's
and into busy Euston Road.

'My girlfriend is coming to London to do her
masters degree in art at the Royal College of Art and
I need this "dream job" if we aren't to be separated,'
he said.

Just passed a red light, missed a turning bus
on the Old Street roundabout, went down City
Road and reached Worship Street, six minutes early.
Overjoyed, they thanked me with a tip. I wished
them luck, then went on my way.

EDGWARE ROAD TO WORSHIP STREET

Every cabbie has a story

I am from Madrid, Spain, a city where we take our food very seriously. We enjoy our social life around the eating table. We eat between 2 p.m. and 4 p.m. for lunch and as late as between 11 p.m. and 2 a.m. for dinner, causing traffic jams as early as 5 a.m. – now isn't that unusual?'

EUSTON STATION
TO PRINCE ALBERT ROAD

● I recall a Spanish passenger who told me a joke in my cab.

'I will tell you a Spanish joke. Once an Englishman came to Madrid and visited one of our restaurants. He couldn't speak much Spanish, so he requested the same meal that a woman who was eating on the next table was having. Fifteen minutes later the waiter returned with the meal. It was worth the wait and he thoroughly enjoyed his meal – so much that he asked what the ingredients were.

'"On the outside of the plate," the waiter said, "is the finest of all Spanish vegetables and in the middle are the balls of a bull from a bullfight."

'The Englishman left a good tip and returned the next night asking for the same meal. This time, it took fifteen minutes longer but it was even tastier than the previous night. He noticed that the balls were smaller. When he asked the waiter why, the waiter replied, "Well, *señor*, sometimes the bull wins!"'

119

Something pinched our bums

'We may look alike but we are not twins, just good friends who sometimes experience bizarre things when we're together.

'Like the other night – we were walking home after a late party, we passed this cemetery, noticed a strange stillness in the air, it was creepy, then something pinched our bums. I thought it was him playing a joke and him me. We looked at each other, realised it wasn't, so we sprinted all the way home without looking back.'

TOTTENHAM COURT ROAD TO MUSWELL HILL

Mickey's first trip to London

'This is Mickey. I got him from a dog rescue centre. The lady who had him was going to throw him out into the street, but now he's with me. He is a great house dog, barks at anything that comes near the house. He is five years old now. He's a cross between a chihuahua and a Yorkshire terrier and loves eating chicken. By the way, it's Mickey's first visit to London.'

EUSTON STATION TO VICTORIA STATION

The Italian lady

'I am from Sorrento, a beautiful small village
on the western coast of Italy.

'My story is about a Spanish queen called Giovenna,
who ruled there. She lived in a palace built on two high
rocks from where she would have her lovers thrown to
their deaths after she finished with them. Her end came
when she was killed by a white horse. Legend has it that
on nights with a full moon the horse and the ghost
queen still wander around, looking for men.

'So … don't go! By the way, my name is Giovenna.'

WIGMORE STREET TO QUEEN'S GATE

In love with the same man?

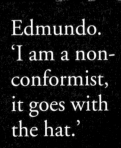

Baby's first time in a cab.

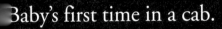

Edmundo.
'I am a non-
conformist,
it goes with
the hat.'

The Norwegian Taff

'I am a Welshman, born in south Wales.
When my father was thirty he got silicosis and
couldn't work any more, and this created a lot
of hardship for my family, so when I was of age
I worked with my grandfather in the mines.

'My father died when he was fifty and I decided
to leave the Welsh valleys and join the British
Army. I was stationed in Germany between
1950 and 1964. In 1964 I represented Great
Britain in the Olympic Games. Then, while
training with the army in Norway, I fell in love
with a woman there and decided to settle down
and have a family.

'I became a ship owner and broke the control
of the cartel in Norway, thanks to the survival
instincts I had learnt as a boy in the mining
valleys of south Wales.

'Now I have five lovely children, two of them
twins. One of them has come with me to visit
London and what a wonderful city it is.'

WATERLOO STATION TO CROMWELL ROAD

I lost 109 chickens in three minutes

'I am from Carmarthen, west Wales, where I enjoy the rural way of life. Where I live there is no GP, no school, no post office, no taxis, no bus and the nearest town is fifteen miles away. I own an organic farm and rear free-range hens. One night last March I heard a rumpus sound coming from my fields. I went to investigate and found five foxes terrorising my hens. By the time I got my dogs, half my chickens were dead, and most of the others were injured and had to be put down. I lost 109 chickens in three minutes and this is not an isolated case. Foxes kill chickens for fun, regardless of whether it's day or night. This accounts for 18 per cent of our stock.'

KENNINGTON ROAD TO PIMLICO

I enjoyed it

'I am seventy-six years old, and I have been smoking a pipe since the age of eighteen.

'As a young man, I wanted people at work to think I was older than I was, so I started smoking a pipe, enjoyed it and have never stopped since.'

WATERLOO STATION TO THE HOUSE OF COMMONS

We often set goals in life

'I work as a medical secretary. I was born in Hackney, my father is from Barbados, my mother from Jamaica.

'When I went to Barbados for the first time, I fell in love with the place. There I met my grandmother for the first time, met cousins I never knew about – it was a nice reunion. Also met my future husband. I've been married now for seven years and have one boy.

'We often set goals in life. I'm happy that I am getting there.'

EUSTON STATION TO HOMERTON HOSPITAL

The faces

These are the cabbies,

The faces of Euston station.

Got to know them

Over the years

When waiting

For their passengers to arrive.

'Frank the Tank' was once an amateur boxer – that's how he got his name. By nature he is a good man and there is nothing he wouldn't do for you. He once foiled a bank robber in Holborn and got shot for his trouble. He has a passion, a love for women, but hasn't found one to love him.

Frank is from Peckham. He's been driving a cab for fifteen years and is divorced with one daughter.

Stewart

Danny is probably the most well-known face at Euston. He has the art of the 'gab' and there is no doubt that whoever travels with him has an experience not to be forgotten. The love of his life is his elderly mother who lives alone in Camden, his two parrots and of course his cab, to which he, like all the other cabbies I know, has a personal attachment.

John

I met up with John, not having seen him for several weeks, on the Euston rank. I was ten cabs behind him and when I arrived I found him trying to remove some chewing gum from his carpet. The incoming train was delayed, and this time the reason given was leaves on the track, so we expected a long wait and an opportunity to catch up on some cab chat.

John began:

'I picked up this elderly gentleman of ninety from King's Cross station. He told me he had been in the merchant navy during the Second World War, had gone to China where he met a girl. Then after the war they got married, where he settled down, lived there through the Chinese Revolution dyeing silk. When his wife died he decided to return to England to visit the country of his birth, having been away for fifty years.

'When I picked him up from King's Cross Station, he had just returned from Southend, the place of his birth. I took him to see where his parents used to live in Putney before they died.

'I stopped in this narrow street because I noticed a blue Jaguar reversing up the street – coming towards us like a snake. I couldn't move out of the way so I started blowing my horn, but he kept coming. There was nothing I could do but brace myself for the inevitable. The car hit us, and the old man jumped out of the cab, waving his stick in disgust at the driver. He told me he would be a witness and offered to give "his honourable declaration" that he saw the accident.

'We eventually got to his destination in Putney. After he had seen his parents' home, I took him to Heathrow airport for a return flight back to China. He gave me some Chinese money and this I found moving – to this very day I treasure it.

'Westminster Insurance wrote to him in China and he replied with his version of the accident. I got a full payout and that was the end of the matter.

'

I have been a cabbie now for forty years, love my job and enjoy meeting people. My father, who is almost ninety, retired recently after being a cabbie for fifty years and I am proud to have followed him in his footsteps.'

The train eventually arrived after a forty-minute delay. John had removed the remaining chewing gum. The first passengers came rushing down the steps. John, who was on point (the front cab in the rank), opened the door, greeted them and got a local job to Russell Square.

'I'll be back in five minutes,' he said.

John lives in a small village in Kent. He has been married for thirty-nine years and has three children.

Mentes

'I had this gentleman, picked him up from Hanover Square, told me he was in a hurry, had fifteen minutes to catch the 5.30 train from King's Cross.

'"I will do my best," I said. So I put my foot down, weaved through the heavy traffic of Regent Street, used all my skill and knowledge of the back streets to get him there. Got there in nine minutes with six minutes to spare, then he says, "Got to go back."

'"What, sir?" I asked.

'"Sorry, cabbie, but I forgot, I came to work by car today."'

Mentes is from Southgate. He's been a cabbie for nine years and he is happily married with three children.

Sandy

'One Saturday night I picked up this smartly dressed man with a 'dicky bow' tie from Conrad's Hotel, Chelsea. He requested Claridge's Hotel so I took him there.

'Going past Victoria he started speaking. "Tell me, do my trousers match my jacket?"

'I turned, switched my light on, looked at his trousers to find he was exposing his private parts to me. Trying to keep my cool, I looked up at him.

'"No, your trousers do not match your jacket," I said. I stopped the cab at the side of the road, turned to him again, and found I hadn't been imagining it. "Get out of my cab, but first clean your hands before you pay your fare." I passed him a Wet One tissue, but he declined to take it. "Keep it in your trousers next time," I said. "What's more, I've seen bigger gherkins."

'He looked embarrassed, threw the money at me, got out of the cab and ran.

'Thought of reporting it to the police but it wasn't worth the hassle.'

Sandy has encountered many bizarre experiences in twelve years of cabbing, but takes it in her stride. She lives in north London, and is married to a cabbie with two lovely children.

Roger Rabbit

Meet 'Roger Rabbit', also known as
Del McCarrick. Over the years I've seen
him at London's mainline stations raising
money for the Leukaemia Research Fund and
also for the Breast Cancer Campaign.
Yet in all this time most of us, including me,
have never seen his face.

In fifteen years Del has completed twenty
marathons, including marathons in New York
and London. Recently he completed a
145-mile race across the Sahara Desert in
which he removed his costume's 3lb head
and tied it to his backpack because of the high
temperatures. In that race he raised £10,000
and to date he has raised £80,000 for the
Leukaemia Research Fund.

Del, who is from the Isle of Sheppey, has
dedicated much of his time to helping others
and amongst us cabbies has gained a lot of
respect for a job well done.

129

George the Greek

'I once picked up this fraud investigator. He was asked by an insurance company to investigate a man who was a bit "iffy" about a medical claim that he had made for his back and spine for £275,000.

'The investigator was told that the man was going on holiday, so he followed him from his home in the Midlands to Victoria station, where he went into the toilet, removed his back brace, put away his fold-up walking sticks in a bag and changed into his beach clothes. After leaving the toilet, he gave the bag to his wife and travelled to the Canary Islands. This man, who was meant to have been disabled by an injury, was filmed jumping off a springboard, donkey riding and, on the last day, bobsleighing down the hotel stairs on a stainless-steel tray.

'When he returned to London, he went to the toilets in Victoria station where he changed back into his usual clothes and back brace and took out his sticks.

'A few weeks later he was asked by the insurance company if he wished to "pursue his claim" and he said "yes". So when the fraud inspector and the insurance solicitor met him, they asked "Would you like to see the video we took of you on holiday?"'

George is married with three children, lives in Edgware and has been driving a cab now for fourteen years.

Den Boy

'I once picked up four blind people plus their dogs from the Victoria and Albert Museum in Kensington.

'One of their dogs had to sit in front, next to me, and I thought nothing more about it.

'We set off and my passengers chatted cheerfully amongst themselves. They even knew when we had crossed Vauxhall Bridge, which I thought was amazing, and I was left in the company of their dog who must have liked me. He was all over me. I tried to restrain him, but couldn't, so I allowed him to lick my face until we got to our destination in Denmark Hill.

'When I got home, my wife noticed I was covered in hairs. She questioned me and asked where I had been.'

Dennis known to fellow cabbies as 'Den Boy' has been driving for twenty years. He lives with his wife and three kids near Shoreditch.

Rip

Rip is a cabbie who is always concerned for others. But like everyone else he's also had his own problems. Unfortunately his problems ran very deep, he turned to alcohol and then we stopped seeing him at Euston station, thought it was the end of him.

But a year later we heard Rip had experienced a little miracle, found himself through Jesus, sorted out his problems and sprung back to life. Rip is now back with us, the same as he was before, but caring for others with a difference. He helps others through various organizations who have drink problems.

Rip now owns a new cab, has moved to a small village near Derby where he spends a lot of time with his wife and three young children.

Bookmark

Nobody at Euston knew who he was, never been known to say a word, always in his cab, his eyes always glued to a book.

Through the years I've watched him read. You can't help noticing the expression on his face, it changes as he turns over the pages – it's just amazing. God knows how many books he's read.

After ten years, I thought it time to introduce myself. I took a photo, he replied with a smile and we had a nice chat. He introduced himself as Mark but as a tribute to our friend 'Frank the Tank' I thought up a name to fit the image of our friend – 'Bookmark'.

Mark is from Essex, is happily married with two kids and has been driving a cab now for over thirteen years.

Lyn

Lyn was one of the first eight ladies
to qualify as a licensed black cab driver
in London. She, like all other cabbies
I know, remembers her very first job.

'It was fifteen years ago, I picked up two
ladies with a roll of carpet from Penton
Street. They wanted to go to Great
Windmill Street and I took them with
this carpet sticking out of the window. I
was as nervous as hell so I used the 38
bus route. As it's customary not to
charge your passengers for your first
job, the ladies walked away very
pleased.'

Lyn is from Islington and is married
with one son.

Mick

Mick's a cheerful cabbie – always gives you
a smile regardless of the weather. He loves
Formula One car racing. I thought he was
joking till one day he left me standing at the
lights in Marylebone Road.

Mick has been cabbing for sixteen years.
He is married with three kids and lives at
Waltham Abbey.

Tall Bob

This is 'Tall Bob', he's 6ft 5in tall.

'What can I say, I'm still waiting after forty minutes for this train to arrive. And when it does, being the kipper season, it will probably be empty.'

Bob is from Mill Hill. He is married with two children and has been a cabbie for thirteen years.

Reg

'Reg the ex-policeman' once picked up a gentleman from Euston and took him to his Chelsea flat. But when they arrived he discovered that this poor gentleman must have had a heart attack and had died. An ambulance was called and his body was taken away. The porter recognised him and telephoned his daughter, who came, and Reg obliged by taking her to the hospital.

Reg is married with two children and one grandchild, and lives happily in Islington. He has been a cabbie for over twenty-seven years.

Steve

'In my thirteen-year career as a London cabbie I have experienced many bizarre and amusing moments. But one that stands out in the memory bank was the day I was hailed by a South American gentleman in Bishopsgate. In broken English he requested to be taken to what sounded like Tooting Common.

'When we duly arrived at our destination, he alighted from the cab with a puzzled expression. "Where is it?" he asked.

'"This is it," I replied.

'"No, the exhibition," he said in an agitated manner.

'"The exhibition?" I queried.

'"The Tutankhamun exhibition," he shouted.

'Thinking quickly to save face, I stated knowingly, "Oh, that exhibition," and ushered him back into the cab. I was unable to stop myself from laughing out loud as I sped him back to the British Museum.'

Steve is from Cheshunt. He has been driving a cab for thirteen years and is married with two children.

Ron the Cap

Here's 'Ron the Cap', out of his cab stretching his legs, eating a Cheddar cheese and onion sandwich which his wife makes for him every morning.

Ron's from Chingford and has been a cabbie for twenty-six years.

Fate

One cold snowy winter's morning, I left home
early, found two old people standing outside
Southgate station. There had been a problem
with the early trains and they needed to get to
Charing Cross station. They got into the cab
and snuggled closely together in the back to
keep warm. We got chatting and I couldn't resist
the temptation to ask how they met.

The old lady's face brightened, like the morning
sun. I knew then I was in for a story.

'You really want to know?'

'Yes, if you don't mind,' I said.

So she started. 'It was before the war. I used
to travel to Oxford by train, passing through
beautiful countryside, little towns and often
empty stations. There was a gentleman I used
to see daily. He'd get on the train, sit in the same
carriage, read his newspaper throughout the
journey and except for the occasional "hello"
and "goodbye" nothing was said. Then, a year
before the war, I stopped seeing him on the
train.

'Then I met someone at a dance, we dated for a
while and got married before he was drafted into
the army and sent to the Far East. He was taken

prisoner by the Japanese and died in a forced labour camp building the Burmese "railway of death". My life was shattered – I just wanted to grieve and I shut myself away from everyone.

'One evening a friend of mine persuaded me to accompany her to a restaurant in a nearby town. I reluctantly accepted, and found it was packed with locals and servicemen on leave trying to forget the war just for a few hours. While waiting to give our order, my friend, Helen, decided to go to the powder room and it was then I noticed a face but could not place it. It then dawned on me it was the person I used to see on the train. Our eyes made contact, and he got up from his table, came over to my table, started talking, told me how by chance he had come with his friends to this restaurant. And we have been together ever since that day.

'We now have three children and six grandchildren. We're about to celebrate our fiftieth anniversary and still very much in love.'

We reached Charing Cross station as the traffic was beginning to build up around Trafalgar Square. I thanked them for the story and as they parted they wished me a 'good life'.

SOUTHGATE STATION TO CHARING CROSS STATION

137

A Christmas story

The lights on the Christmas tree in Trafalgar Square had just been switched on. I was taking a few photos of the tree when two young women appeared, asked me if I would take a fare to Marylebone Road and then on to Paddington station. I agreed, put my camera away, put on my hire light and off we went. After passing Piccadilly Circus, I noticed that one of my passengers, a blonde, was from England, the other who had black hair was from the USA. We got chatting, something cabbies like doing. The American lady told me she was married.

'Yes,' I said. 'You have been married for about three years.'

'Two and a half years to be exact, but how did you guess that?'

'I didn't,' I replied.

'What's more you'll be having your first baby next year.'

They looked at each other in amazement and started laughing. When we dropped her friend off in Marylebone Road, we continued the conversation.

'Nobody at work knows I'm pregnant.'

I then looked into my mirror and gave her a smile.

'So please tell me cabbie, how did you know?'

'Psychic awareness, madam,' but she was not convinced.

'Please tell me, how did you do it?'

'I do it all the time,' I replied.

We arrived at Paddington, she paid me, gave me a £2 coin as a tip. 'Merry Christmas, cabbie.'

'Merry Christmas, madam, and if I may say so I think you will be a good mother.'
She turned, gave me a nice smile and rushed off to get the train. Probably I shouldn't open my mouth because one day it might get me into trouble, but that would be boring, I thought.

TRAFALGAR SQUARE TO PADDINGTON STATION VIA MARYLEBONE ROAD

There was a long queue on the Paddington rank, so I decided to do one more job before packing it up for the day. My passengers, a young couple, wanted the Savoy Hotel. As we went down Park Lane, I switched on my microphone, then said, 'Good evening, folks, welcome to London, hope you enjoy your honeymoon.'

They looked at each other, then turned to me and said, 'How did you know that?'

PADDINGTON STATION TO THE
SAVOY HOTEL, SAVOY COURT

Time is an old friend
Of mine.
It's like the wind,
Here one moment
Gone the next,
But I won't forget you,
Time has told me not to.

Was a time
When I found myself lost,
Deep in the pain of my soul,
Found myself
Fighting for my life,
With the cloak of death
That had come
To collect me,
For a fate
That was to await me.

It was in
The darkness of my life
Saw a light
Burnt so bright,
Like a vision,
Like an angel
Sent from heaven.
She came,
Took me by the hand,
Back to that light
That burnt so bright
In the darkness of
That cold night.

It was in the morning
Of my life,
Found myself
High up
In the mountains,
Beneath lay cotton wool
Cushions of white clouds
That stretched far
Into the infinity
Of the coral blue skies.
Could hear the music
Of the birds,
And river streams,
Mingle with the sweetness
Of spring that was
In the air.
Felt a warmth
Within me,
Realised she was
Beside me.

We talked of life,
Talked of love,
Time stood still,
Then a gentle
Breeze
Blew against my face.
Closed my eyes
For a moment,
When I opened them
She was gone …

Things have changed

In our lives.

Yesterday is history,

Tomorrow is a mystery,

Today is a gift.

It's spring again

Here in London.

The morning sun is rising

Over Tavistock Square.

The child we first saw

Has grown and begun to walk

And passes beneath

The Tree of Peace

In the trail

Of her mother's footsteps.

How beautiful life is.

I look at my watch

Gone 9.40.

Got to get going.

I quickly finish my coffee,

Switch on my hire light.

Get to Euston Station.

Find a long queue of people

Waiting for cabs.

Who will I meet today?

What will I hear?

Where will the journey

Take me?

Now that's another story …

First published in Great Britain in 2003 by
Orion Media
An imprint of Orion Books Ltd
Orion House, 5 Upper St Martin's Lane,
London WC2H 9EA

A CIP catalogue record for this book
is available from the British Library

ISBN 0 75285 618 9

Printed in Italy by Printers Trento srl